# Banking in India

## Past, Present and Future

# Banking in India

## Past, Present and Future

*By*

Ujjwala Shahi

Associate Professor,
B.D. College, Magadh University, Patna

New Century Publications
New Delhi, India

NEW CENTURY PUBLICATIONS
4852 / 24, 1st Floor,
Ansari Road, Daryaganj,
New Delhi – 110 002 (India)

Tel.: 011-4101 7798; 4358 7398; 98112 66355
E-mail: info@newcenturypublications.com

**www.newcenturypublications.com**

*Editorial office:*
4800 / 24, Bharat Ram Road,
Ansari Road, Daryaganj,
New Delhi – 110 002



**Edition: 2026**

ISBN: **978-81-7708-334-7**

Published by New Century Publications and printed at Milan Enterprises, New Delhi.

Designs: Patch Creative Unit, New Delhi.

PRINTED IN INDIA

यू.के. सिन्हा
अध्यक्ष
**U. K. Sinha**
Chairman

भारतीय प्रतिभूति और विनिमय बोर्ड
SECURITIES AND EXCHANGE BOARD OF INDIA

## Foreword

Dr. Ujjwala Shahi belongs to an illustrious family of Bihar whom I know for more than three decades. It was a great pleasure when I received the request to write the foreword for her book on banking.

Banking sector is the backbone of Indian economy. Bank credit accounts for more than two-third of GDP in India. Banks also account for the largest share of households financial savings in India. More than 42 % of households financial savings in India gets deposited in commercial banks and another 5 % in NBFCs and co-operative banks. Apart from the traditional function of taking deposits and giving credit, banking in India has played a larger role in economic and social emancipation of India through priority sector lending, expansion of branches to rural areas, partnering social welfare programmes of the Government such as Prime Minister Rojgar Yojana, Indira Aawas Yojana and the more recent National Rural Employment Guarantee Act (NREGA). The dominance of well regulated public sector banks, in a way, has also contributed to the stability to Indian financial system during challenging times.

Moving ahead, some of the emerging issues and challenges in the Indian banking space include improving the capital adequacy requirements as per Basel III Norms, adjusting to changes in policy rates to maintain economic stability, managing non-performing assets, enhancing sales & services standards, improving organisation design and using innovative technology through new channels. Despite this, there are several positives like the high population base of India, advent of mobile banking, enhanced financial inclusion, rising disposable income, etc. that can reasonably be expected to drive the growth of Indian banking industry in the long run.

In the above context, this book seems well timed. The book has a comprehensive coverage of various banks in India and their evolution over the years. I am sure the book will serve as a good reference on the Indian banking sector. The section on financial inclusion, which touches upon inclusion models in other countries, is a valuable addition in the book. I compliment the author for being able to put together a vast wealth of information on the Indian banking sector into a concise book.

UKSinha

**U. K. Sinha**

सेबी भवन, प्लॉट सं.सी 4-ए, "जी" ब्लॉक, बांद्रा-कुर्ला कॉम्प्लेक्स, बांद्रा (पूर्व), मुंबई - 400 051. • दूरभाष : 2644 9999 / 4045 9999
फैक्स : 2644 9003 • ई-मेल : chairman@sebi.gov.in • वेब : www.sebi.gov.in

SEBI Bhavan, Plot No. C4-A, "G" Block, Bandra Kurla Complex, Bandra (E), Mumbai - 400 051. • Tel.: 2644 9999 / 4045 9999
Fax : 2644 9003 • E-mail : chairman@sebi.gov.in • Web : www.sebi.gov.in

# About the Book

Banking in India has a long history and it has evolved over the years passing through various phases. The beginning of modern day banking in India can be traced to 18th century when English traders came to India. The English Agency Houses in Calcutta and Bombay began to conduct banking business besides their commercial activities.

Banking in India during the pre-Independence period was largely characterised by the existence of private banks organised as joint stock companies. Most banks were small and had private shareholding of the closely-held variety. They were largely localised and many of them failed.

At the time of Independence in 1947, the Indian banking system was weak. The entire banking sector was in the private sector and the credit requirements of agriculture and other needy sectors were ignored. With a view to better aligning the banking system to the needs of planning and economic policy, the policy of social control over the banking sector began in 1967. The year 1969 was a landmark in the history of commercial banking in India. In July of that year, the Government nationalised 14 major commercial banks of the country. In April 1980, Government nationalised 6 more commercial banks.

The period beginning from the early 1990s witnessed the transformation of the banking sector as a result of financial sector reforms that were introduced as a part of structural reforms initiated in 1991.

This book integrates and brings together the history of modern banking in India, with focus on recent developments in the context of liberalization and privatization wave sweeping across world economies.

# Author's Profile

**Dr. Ujjwala Shahi** is currently an Associate Professor, B.D. College, Magadh University, Patna. A historian by profession, she has been teaching modern Indian history since 1984.

She did her B.A. from Patna University and M.A. and Ph.D. in history from Bihar University. She has been contributing to national newspapers and in-house magazines on a regular basis. She has interviewed famous personalities on Doordarshan and delivered talks on All India Radio.

# Contents

# Preface

The origin of banking in India can be traced back to the Vedic period. The transformation from pure money lending to proper banking appears to have taken place before the times of Manu. Money lending in one form or the other has evolved along with the history of mankind. Indian history is also replete with instances referring to indigenous money lenders, *Sahukars* and *Zamindars* involved in the business of money lending and lending by mortgaging landed property of the borrowers. The beginning of modern day banking in India can be traced to 18th century when English traders came to India. The English Agency Houses in Calcutta and Bombay began to conduct banking business besides their usual commercial activities.

Banking in India during the pre-Independence period was largely characterised by the existence of private banks organised as joint stock companies. Most banks were small and had private shareholding of the closely-held variety. They were largely localised and many of them failed.

In 1806, the Bank of Calcutta was established as a joint stock bank with limited liability, which was brought under the Royal Charter in 1809 and renamed as Bank of Bengal. Subsequently, the Bank of Bombay and the Bank of Madras were established by the East India Company in 1840 and 1843 respectively. The business of these Presidency banks were initially confined to discounting of bills or other negotiable private securities, keeping cash accounts, receiving deposits, and issuing and circulating cash notes.

Banks came under the purview of the Reserve Bank of India (RBI) that was established as a central bank for the country in 1935. However, the process of regulation and supervision was limited by the provisions of the RBI Act, 1934 and the Companies Act, 1913. The indigenous bankers and moneylenders had remained mainly isolated from the institutional part of the system. The usurious network was still rampant and exploitative. Co-operative credit was the only hope for credit in rural areas but the movement was successful only in a few regions.

As in several other developing countries, the financial system in India has traditionally been dominated by financial intermediaries, especially banking institutions. Banking in India has a long history and it has evolved over the years passing through various phases. At the time of Independence, the Indian banking system was weak. The entire banking sector was in the private sector and the credit requirements of agriculture and other needy sectors were ignored.

With a view to better aligning the banking system to the needs of planning and economic policy, the policy of social control over the banking sector began in 1967. The year 1969 was a landmark in the history of commercial banking in India. In July of that year, the government nationalised 14 major commercial banks of the country. In April 1980, government nationalised 6 more commercial banks. Leading commercial banks of the country were nationalised with the following objectives in view: (a) to break the ownership and control of banks by a few business families, (b) to prevent concentration of wealth and economic power, (c) to mobilise savings of the masses from every nook and corner of the country, and (d) to pay greater attention to the credit needs of the priority sectors like agriculture and small industries.

The period beginning from the early 1990s witnessed the transformation of the banking sector as a result of financial sector reforms that were introduced as a part of structural reforms initiated in 1991. The reform process in the financial sector was undertaken with the prime objective of having a strong and resilient banking system. The progress achieved in the areas of strengthening the regulatory and supervisory norms has ushered in greater accountability and market discipline amongst the participants. The RBI has made sustained efforts towards adoption of international benchmarks in a gradual manner, as appropriate to the Indian conditions, in various areas such as prudential norms, risk management, supervision, corporate governance and transparency and disclosures. The reform process has helped in taking the management of the banking sector to the level, where the RBI ceased to micro-manage commercial banks and focused largely on the macro goals. The focus on deregulation and liberalisation coupled with enhanced responsibilities for banks made the banking sector resilient and capable of facing several newer global challenges.

This book is intended to integrate and bring together the history and the role of various players in modern day banking in India.

I express my gratitude to the Principal of B.D. College, Shri B.N. Ojha for extending much needed support and help for completion of this book. I would also like to acknowledge the tremendous amount of support, understanding and motivation which was provided by my husband, Shri Sushil Kumar Mishra, who has been with me all through the making of this book since inception. Thanks are also due to my entire family, including my mother-in-law Shrimati Sumitra Mishra and my parents Shri L.P. Shahi and Shrimati Madhuri Shahi, and my children Dr. Ruchika Mishra and Khushi Mishra and Manu Rao, for their love and support.

Patna **Ujjwala Shahi**

*September 2012*

# 1

# Banking in India: An Introduction

In ancient times, religious temples used to be the abode not only for Gods but also for gold and jewellery. Temples were regarded to be the safest place to store gold as they were constantly attended, were well-built and were sacred, thus deterring thieves. There are even records from 18th century BC Babylon, of loans that were made by temple priests to merchants.

Ancient Greece also provides evidence of banking. Greek temples as well as private and civic entities conducted financial transactions such as loans, deposits, currency exchange, and validation of coinage. There is evidence too of credit, whereby in return for a payment from a client, a money lender in one Greek port would write a credit note for the client who could "cash" the note in another city, saving the client the danger of carting coinage with him on his journey.

Ancient Rome perfected the administrative aspect of banking and saw greater regulation of financial institutions and financial practices. Charging interest on loans and paying interest on deposits became more highly developed and competitive.

The origin of banking in India can be traced back to almost the Vedic period. The transformation from pure money lending to proper banking appears to have taken place before the time of Manu. Manu had devoted a section of his work explaining the deposits and advances and he even laid down certain rules on rates of interest.

Throughout the Maryann period and later on, desi bankers played a role in the economy of the country. However, it was during the Mughal period that indigenous bankers started playing a vital role in lending money and financing foreign trade and commerce.

Later on, prior to the establishment of banks, financial activities were handled by money lenders and individuals. This period was marked by very high interest rates. There was lack of security of public savings and no uniformity regarding loans.

## 1.1 Advent of Banking in India

The English traders who came to India in the 18th century could not make much use of the indigenous bankers, owing to their ignorance of the language as well as the inexperience of the European trade by the local people. The English Agency Houses in Calcutta and Bombay began to conduct banking business besides their commercial business.

The Europeans with aptitude of commercial pursuit, who resigned from civil and military, organized these agency houses. A type of business organization recognizable as managing agency took form in the period from 1834 to 1847.

The primary concern of these agency houses was trade, but they branched out into banking as a sideline to facilitate the operations of their main business.

The English agency houses that began to serve as bankers to the East India Company had no capital of their own, and depended on deposits for their funds. They financed movement of crops, issued paper money and established joint stock banks.

Banking in India originated in the last decades of the 18th century. The first banks were The General Bank of India, which started in 1786, and Bank of Hindustan, which started in 1790, both of which are now defunct. In the first half of the 19th century, three Presidency banks were founded. The oldest bank in existence in India is the State Bank of India, which originated as the Bank of Calcutta in June 1806, which almost immediately became the Bank of Bengal. This was one of the three Presidency banks, the other two being the Bank of Bombay (1840) and the Bank of Madras (1843). All three of them were established under charters from the British East India Company. For many years the Presidency banks acted as quasi-central banks, as did their successors.

The beginning of the 20th century saw the introduction of joint stock banks. In 1921, the Presidency banks were merged together to form the Imperial Bank of India, which was subsequently renamed the State Bank of India in 1955. In 1935, India's central bank, the Reserve Bank of India (RBI), began operations. Following Independence, the RBI was given broad regulatory authority over commercial banks in India. In 1959, the State Bank of India acquired the state-owned banks of eight former princely States. Thus, by July 1969, approximately 31 percent of scheduled bank branches throughout India were government controlled, as part of the State Bank of India.

## 1.2 Banking Defined

A bank is an organization, usually a corporation, chartered by a state or federal government, which does most or all of the following: receives demand deposits and time deposits, honours instruments drawn on it, and pays interest on deposits with it; discounts notes, makes loans, and invests in securities; collects cheques, drafts, and notes; certifies depositor's cheques; and issues drafts and cashier's cheques. It can also be said to be a financial institution that accepts deposits and channels the money into lending and investment activities.

Banks in India are regulated by the Banking Regulation Act, 1949. It may be mentioned that the Banking Regulation Act, 1949 is not applicable to a primary agricultural society, a cooperative land mortgage bank and any other cooperative society except in the manner and to the extent specified in Part V of the Act. Some banks are included in the Second Schedule to the Reserve Bank of India Act, 1934; these are called scheduled banks. The Reserve Bank includes a bank in this schedule if it fulfils certain conditions.

The Reserve Bank gives certain facilities to scheduled

banks including the following: (a) the purchase, sale, and re-discounting of certain bills of exchange, or promissory notes; (b) purchase and sale of foreign exchange; (c) purchase, sale and re-discounting of foreign bills of exchange; (d) making of loans and advances to scheduled Banks; (e) maintenance of accounts of the scheduled bank in its banking department and issue department; (f) remittance of money between different branches of scheduled banks through the offices, branches or agencies of Reserve Bank free of cost or at nominal rates.

Banking is the business activity of accepting and safeguarding money owned by other individuals and entities, and then lending out this money in order to earn a profit. The Banking activities in India are regulated by the Banking Regulation Act, 1949. Under Section 5(b) of the said Act "Banking" means, the accepting, for the purpose of lending or investment, of deposits of money from the public, repayable on demand or otherwise, and withdrawal by cheque, draft, order or otherwise. Any bank which transacts this business in India is called a banking company. However, any company which is engaged in the manufacture of goods or carries on any trade and which accepts deposits of money from the public merely for the purpose of financing its business as manufacturer or trader shall not be deemed to transact the business of banking.

Section 6 of the Banking Regulation Act, 1949 specifies the forms of business in which a Banking company may engage. These are: (i) borrowing, raising or taking up of money; lending or advancing of money; drawing, making, accepting, discounting, buying, selling, collecting and dealing in bills of exchange, hundies, promissory notes, etc.; (ii) acting as agents for any government or local authority or any other person; (iii) providing for public and private loans (iv) effecting, insuring, guaranteeing, under-writing, participating in managing and carrying out of any issue of shares, stock, debentures, etc.; (v) carrying on and transacting every kind of guarantee and indemnity business; (vi) managing, selling and realizing property which may come into the possession of the banking company in satisfaction of its claim; (vii) acquiring and holding and generally dealing with any property or any right, title or interest in such property which may form the security for any loans and advances; (viii) underwriting and executing trusts; (ix) establishing and supporting or aiding in the establishment and support of institutions, funds, trusts etc. (x) acquisition, construction, maintenance and alteration of any building and works necessary for the purpose of the banking company; (xi) selling, improving, managing, developing, exchanging, leasing, mortgaging, depositing of or turning into account or otherwise dealing with all or any part of the property and rights of the company; (xii) acquiring and undertaking whole or any part of the business of any person or company; (xiii) doing all such other things as are incidental or conducive to the promotion or advancement of the business of the banking company; (xiv) any other business which the Central Government may specify by notification in the Official Gazette. No banking company shall engage in any form of business other than those referred to above.

### 1.3 Functions of Commercial Banks

The functions of a commercial bank can be segregated into three main areas.

**1.3.1 Payment System:** Banks are at the core of the payments system in an economy. A payment refers to the means by which financial transactions are settled. A fundamental method by which banks help in settling the financial transaction process is by issuing and paying cheques issued on behalf of customers. Further, in modern banking, the payments system also involves electronic banking, wire transfers, settlement of credit card transactions, etc. In all such transactions, banks play a critical role.

**1.3.2 Financial Intermediation:** The second principal function of a bank is to take different types of deposits from customers and then lend these funds to borrowers, in other words, financial intermediation. In financial terms, bank deposits represent the banks' liabilities, while loans disbursed, and investments made by banks are their assets. Bank deposits serve the useful purpose of addressing the needs of depositors, who want to ensure liquidity, safety, as well as returns in the form of interest. On the other hand, bank loans and investments made by banks play an important function in channelling funds into profitable as well as socially productive uses.

**1.3.3 Financial Services:** In addition to acting as financial intermediaries, banks today are increasingly involved with offering customers a wide variety of financial services including investment banking, insurance-related services, government-related business, foreign exchange businesses, wealth management services, etc. Income from providing such services improves a bank's profitability.

## 1.4 Financial Intermediaries

Banks face competition from a wide range of financial intermediaries in the public and private sectors in the areas of financial intermediation and financial services (although the payments system is exclusively for banks). Such intermediaries form a diverse group in terms of size and nature of their activities, and play an important role in the financial system by not only competing with banks, but also complementing them in providing a wide range of financial services.

Some of these intermediaries include the following:

**1.4.1 Term-lending Institutions:** Term-lending institutions exist at both state and all-India levels. They provide term loans (i.e., loans with medium to long-term maturities) to various industry, service and infrastructure sectors for setting up new projects and for the expansion of existing facilities and there by compete with banks. At the all-India level, these institutions are typically specialized, catering to the needs of specific sectors, which make them competitors to banks in those areas. These include the Export Import Bank of India (EXIM Bank), Small Industries Development Bank of India (SIDBI), Tourism Finance Corporation of India Limited (TFCI), and Power Finance Corporation Limited (PFCL). A notable exception is Industrial Finance Corporation of India Ltd. (IFCI), which lends to a variety of sectors. At the state level, various State Financial Corporations (SFCs) have been set up to finance and promote small and medium-sized enterprises. There are also State Industrial Development Corporations (SIDCs), which provides finance primarily to medium-sized and large-sized enterprises. In addition to SFCs and SIDCs, the North Eastern Development Financial Institution Ltd. (NEDFI) has been set up to cater specifically to the needs of the north-eastern states.

**1.4.2 Non-banking Financial Companies (NBFCs):** India has many thousands of non-banking financial companies, predominantly from the private sector. NBFCs are required to register with RBI in terms of the Reserve Bank of India (Amendment) Act, 1997. The principal activities of NBFCs include equipment-leasing, hire purchase, loan and investment and asset finance.

NBFCs have been competing with and complementing the services of commercial banks for a long time. All NBFCs together currently account for around nine percent of assets of the total financial system in India. Housing finance companies form a distinct sub-group of the NBFCs.

As a result of some recent government incentives for investing in the housing sector, business of these companies has grown substantially. Housing Development Finance Corporation Limited (HDFC), which is in the private sector and the Government-controlled Housing and Urban Development Corporation Limited (HUDCO) are the two premier housing finance companies. These companies are major players in the mortgage business, and provide stiff competition to commercial banks in the disbursal of housing loans.

**1.4.3 Insurance Companies:** Insurance/reinsurance companies such as Life Insurance Corporation of India (LIC), General Insurance Corporation of India (GIC), and others provide substantial long-term financial assistance to the industrial and housing sectors and to that extent, are competitors of banks. LIC is the biggest player in this area.

**1.4.4 Mutual Funds:** Mutual funds offer competition to banks in the area of fund mobilization, in that they offer alternate routes of investment to households. Most mutual funds are standalone asset management companies. In addition, a number of banks, both in the private and public sector have sponsored asset management companies to undertake mutual fund business. Banks have thus entered the asset management business, sometimes on their own and other times in joint venture with others.

## 1.5 Structure of Banking in India

**1.5.1 Banking Regulator:** The Reserve Bank of India (RBI) is the central banking and monetary authority of India, and also acts as the regulator and supervisor of commercial Banks.

**1.5.2 Scheduled Banks in India:** Scheduled banks comprise scheduled commercial banks and scheduled cooperative banks. Scheduled commercial banks form the bedrock of the Indian financial system, currently accounting for more than three-fourth assets of all financial institutions. SCBs are present throughout India, and their branches have grown more than four-fold in the last 40 years.

**1.5.3 Public Sector Banks:** Public sector banks are those in which the majority stake is held by the Government of India (GoI). Public sector banks together make up the largest category in the Indian banking system. There are currently 26 public sector banks in India. They include the SBI and its 5 associate banks (such as State Bank of Hyderabad, State Bank of Bikaner & Jaipur etc.), 19 nationalized banks (such as Allahabad Bank, Canara Bank, etc.) and IDBI Bank Ltd.

Public sector banks have taken the lead role in branch expansion, particularly in the rural areas.

**1.5.4 Regional Rural Banks:** Regional rural banks (RRBs) were established during 1976-1987 with a view to develop the rural economy. Each RRB is owned jointly by the Central Government, State Government concerned and a sponsoring public sector commercial Bank. RRBs provide credit to small farmers, artisans, small entrepreneurs and agricultural labourers. Over the years, the Government has introduced a number of measures to improve viability and profitability of RRBs, one of them being the amalgamation of the RRBs of the same sponsor bank within a State.

**1.5.5 Private Sector Banks:** In this type of banks, the majority of share capital is held by private individuals and corporates. Not all private sector banks were nationalized in 1969 and 1980. The private banks which were not nationalized are collectively known as the old private sector banks and include banks such as The Jammu and Kashmir Bank Ltd., Lord Krishna Bank Ltd, etc. Entry of private sector banks was, however, prohibited during the post-Nationalization period. In July 1993, as part of the banking reform process and as a measure to induce competition in the banking sector, RBI permitted the private sector to enter into the banking system. This resulted in the creation of a new set of private sector banks, which are collectively known as the new private sector banks.

**1.5.6 Foreign Banks:** Foreign banks have their registered and head offices in a foreign country but operate their branches in India. The RBI permits these banks to operate either through branches; or through wholly-owned subsidiaries. The primary activity of most foreign banks in India has been in the corporate segment. However, some of the larger foreign banks have also made consumer financing as a significant part of their portfolios. These banks offer products such as automobile finance, home loans, credit cards, household consumer finance, etc. Foreign banks in India are required to adhere to all banking regulations, including priority-sector lending norms as applicable to domestic banks. In addition to the entry of the new private banks in the mid-1990s, the increased presence of foreign banks in India has also contributed to boosting competition in the banking sector.

**1.5.7 Cooperative Banks:** Cooperative banks cater to the financing needs of agriculture, retail trade, small industry and self-employed businessmen in urban, semi-urban and rural areas of India. A distinctive feature of the cooperative credit structure in India is its heterogeneity. The structure differs across urban and rural areas, across states and loan maturities. Urban areas are served by urban cooperative Banks (UCBs), whose operations are either limited to one state or stretch across states. The rural cooperative banks comprise state cooperative banks, district central cooperative banks, SCARDBs and PCARDBs (SCARDB stands for State Cooperative Agricultural and Rural Development Bank and PCARDB stands for Primary Cooperative Agricultural and Rural Development Bank). The cooperative banking sector is the oldest segment of the Indian banking system.

## 1.6 Role of Reserve Bank of India

As the central bank of the country, the RBI performs a wide range of functions like:

1. It acts as the currency authority.
2. It controls money supply and credit.
3. It manages foreign exchange.
4. It serves as a banker to the government.
5. It builds up and strengthens the country's financial infrastructure.
6. It acts as the banker to banks.
7. It supervises banks.

To ensure a sound banking system in the country, the RBI exercises powers of supervision, regulation and control over commercial banks. RBI's regulatory functions relating to banks cover their establishment (i.e. licensing), branch expansion, liquidity of their assets, management and methods of working, amalgamation, reconstruction and liquidation. RBI controls the commercial banks through periodic inspection of banks and follow-up action and by calling for returns and other information from them, besides holding periodic meetings with the top management of the banks. RBI also performs its role as the banker to the government, under which the RBI conducts the Government's market borrowing programme.

# 2

# Reserve Bank of India (RBI)

## 2.1 Origins of the Reserve Bank of India

The origin of the Reserve Bank of India can be traced to 1926, when the Royal Commission on Indian Currency and Finance—also known as the Hilton-Young Commission—recommended the creation of a central bank to separate the control of currency and credit from the government and to augment Banking facilities throughout the country. The Reserve Bank of India Act of 1934 established the Reserve Bank as the banker to the central government and set in motion a series of actions culminating in the start of operations w.e.f 1st April, 1935. Starting as a private shareholders' bank, the Reserve Bank was nationalized in 1949. It then assumed the responsibility to meet the aspirations of a newly independent country and its people. The Reserve Bank's nationalization was aimed at achieving coordination between the policies of the government and those of the central bank. Since then, the Reserve Bank's role and functions have undergone numerous changes—as the nature of the Indian economy changed.

The Preamble to the Reserve Bank of India Act, 1934 (the Act), under which it was constituted, specifies its objective as "to regulate the issue of bank notes and the keeping of reserves with a view to securing monetary stability in India and generally to operate the currency and credit system of the country to its advantage".

As evident from the multifaceted functions the Reserve Bank performs today, its role and priorities have changed with changing national priorities and global developments. Reserve Bank has demonstrated dynamism and flexibility to meet the requirements of an evolving economy.

**Box 2.1: An Anecdote of Art, Central Bank, and Philistines**

On achieving Independence, the government planned a number of public buildings to house the institutions of independent India. In this context, Pandit Jawaharlal Nehru, the Prime Minister, suggested that public buildings, many of which were large imposing structures, could be utilized to 'encourage Indian artists to function in some way' and sculptors, painters, designers, etc. could be asked to cooperate. Nehru opined that the art work '...should cost very little in comparison with the total cost of the buildings. But it will encourage Indian artists and would be greatly welcomed, I think, by the public'. The Finance Secretary, Shri K.G. Ambegaokar, sent a copy of the note to B. Rama Rau, the then Governor. This was the time when the Reserve Bank was in the process of constructing/contemplating new buildings at New Delhi, Madras and Nagpur. Accordingly, the Bank set up a committee consisting of Shri J.D. Gondhalekar, Dean of the J.J. School of Arts, Bombay, Shri G.M. Bhuta of M/s Master, Sathe and Bhuta and Shri R.D. Pusalkar, Assistant Chief Accountant of the Bank to examine the proposal and to make recommendations on the subject.

Amongst other schemes, the Committee recommended that sculptures could be erected on either side of the main entrance of the RBI office at New Delhi, one depicting the idea of "prosperity through industry" and the other "prosperity through agriculture". At the instance of J.R.D. Tata, the then Director of the Central Board, the views of Carl Khandalawalla, an eminent critic and connoisseur of art, were sought. It was he who suggested that the Bank could consider having figures of "Yaksha" and "Yakshini" on the two sides. On his advice, the invitation to tender for the adornment of the frontage of the New Delhi Office was extended to the nine artists.

Out of the nine artists invited, five submitted their proposals and amongst them only one submitted models and sketches. The proposal of Shri Ram Kinkar Baij was accepted. The art form of the male 'Yaksha' was drawn from the statue of the 'Parkham Yaksha' in the Mathura museum and the art form of the female Yakshini was derived from "Bisnagar Yakshini" from the Calcutta Museum. Shri Khandalawalla felt that these massive figures would go very well with the architectural features of RBI New Delhi office.

Contd...

While the themes of peasant-worker prosperity drew upon Nehru's 'scientific temper', its manifestation in the form of the Yaksha and Yakshani appealed to the sensibilities of those steeped in tradition - according to Hindu mythology Yakshas belong to a class of demi-gods and they are represented as the servants of 'Kubera' the God of Wealth. The duty of Yakshas is to guard Kuber's gardens and treasures. The Yakshini is a female Yaksha. The Bank by virtue of it having the sole right of note issue and being a Banker to the Central and State Government could, therefore, be compared with Kubera- the lord of wealth and the statues of the Yaksha and Yakshini could assume the duty of guarding the Bank's treasure. In the modern context, the figures could also be given the allegorical interpretations of symbolising industry and agriculture, subject matters with which the Bank as a Central Bank of the country was directly or indirectly concerned.

Art, Central Bank, and Philistines 1

Art, Central Bank, and Philistines 2

The saga of the sculptures exercised the Bank officials for quite a while as the artist, Ram Kinker, took his own time in selecting the exact quality of stone that was needed which entailed exploration of sites, stone quality, problems in its quarrying and transportation to New Delhi.

Contd...

The work was subject to very considerable delay and on many an occasion the Bank felt that the while Shri Ram Kinker may be possessed of excellent artistic merit, he perhaps did not have the management skills to undertake the enterprise. By the time the sculptures were ready chiselled and polished around December 1966 (January, 1967), the original estimates had to undergo a considerable revision.

That, however, was not the end of the story. When the statues were finally installed, it was over ten years since they had been commissioned; in the meanwhile, the times and circumstances, and the outlook of the country and its leaders had changed. The statues, when being installed at the Reserve Bank's New Delhi Office at Parliament Street, did seem to offend the prudish sensibilities of parts of the populace; the specific cause of provocation was the statue of the Yakshini, depicted in her natural beauty.

The issue of the statues was raised rather starkly in the Rajya Sabha by Prof. Satyavrata Siddhantalankar:

'Will the Minster of Works and Housing and Supply be pleased to state:

1. Is it a fact that the statue of a naked woman has been erected in front of the Reserve Bank of India, Parliament Street and
2. If so what is the object in erecting this statue of a naked woman?'

An exegesis that the 'naked woman' was essentially an allegorical interpretation, representing agriculture and wealth was perhaps convincing though not without further supplementary questions regarding costs incurred and the details of the committee who recommended the art.

While the cause of disquiet generally was the Yakshani, the popular weekly tabloid, Blitz, certainly not prudish in its outlook or ill informed of art, characteristically put an entirely different angle to the statues and likened the Yaksha to resemble Sadoba Patil, an industrialist. Against the title "Yaksha Patil", Blitz depicted a photograph of the statue and commented "...But artist Ram Kinker's conception of a modern Yaksha, which now guards the Reserve Bank, has, coincidentally enough, taken an amazing likeness to Sadoba Patil, one of the most zealous 'guardians' of wealth and big business in the country…".

Contd…

In the wake of the Blitz article, it was felt that the misunderstandings the statues gave rise to could perhaps be addressed by issuing a suitable Press Comminique and issuing hand outs on the art the Bank had commissioned; alternately it was felt that issuing handouts and communiqués would once again revive the controversies. The consensus finally veered in favour of silence. The early nineteen fifties, when Pandit Nehru had conceived the idea of encouraging art, were an era of optimism, different from the lean period of the sixties when, art had, perhaps, to be relegated to the background. Governor P.C. Bhattacharyya, perhaps had his fingers on the pulse when he remarked "Let sleeping dogs lie! Neither the decision to spend the money nor the delay associated with the execution of the project can be justified in the present day context. It would be equally futile to explain through a press note the symbolic significance of the figures put up. We can deal with any question that may be asked in Parliament on an ad hoc basis".

A core function of the Reserve Bank has been the formulation and implementation of monetary policy with the objectives of maintaining price stability and ensuring adequate flow of credit to productive sectors of the economy. In addition to this, the goal of maintaining financial stability was also added. The objective of maintaining financial stability has spanned its role from external account management to oversight of banks and non-banking financial institutions as also of money, government securities and foreign exchange markets.

The Reserve Bank initiates, plans and implements the regulatory policies for banking and non-banking financial institutions with the aim of providing people access to the banking system, protecting depositors' interest, and maintaining the overall health of the financial system. Its function of regulating the commercial banking sector, which emerged with the enactment of the Banking Regulation Act, 1949, has been expanded to cover other entities also. Amendments to the Banking Regulation Act, 1949 brought cooperative Banks and regional rural banks under the Reserve Bank's jurisdiction, while amendments to the Reserve Bank of

India Act saw development finance institutions, non-banking financial companies and primary dealers coming under its regulation, as these entities became important players in the financial system and markets. The global economic uncertainties during and after the Second World War called for conservation of scarce foreign exchange reserves. Initially, the Reserve Bank carried out the regulation of foreign exchange transactions under the Defence of India Rules, 1939 and later, under the Foreign Exchange Regulation Act of 1947. Now the role has shifted from foreign exchange regulation to foreign exchange management.

Post-Independence, as the emerging nation tried to meet the aspirations of a large and diversified populace, the Reserve Bank was entrusted with a variety of developmental roles. With the onset of economic planning in 1950-51, the Reserve Bank undertook a variety of developmental functions to encourage savings and capital formation and widen and deepen the agricultural and industrial credit set-up. The strategy for nearly four decades placed emphasis on the state-induced or state-supported developmental efforts. Subsequently, the role of the financial sector and financial markets was also given an explicit recognition in the development strategy.

The approach under the reforms era i.e. post-1991 included a thrust towards liberalisation, privatisation, globalisation and concerted efforts at strengthening the existing and emerging institutions and market participants. The Reserve Bank adopted international best practices in areas, such as, prudential regulation, banking technology, monetary policy instruments, external sector management and currency management to make the new policy framework effective.

The rapid pace of growth achieved by the financial system in the deregulated regime necessitated a deepening and widening of access to banking services. The new millennium has seen the Reserve Bank play an active role in balancing the relationship between banks and customers; focusing on financial inclusion; setting up administrative machinery to handle customer grievances; pursuing clean note policy and ensuring development and oversight of secure and robust payment and settlement systems.

The last two decades have also seen growing integration of the national economy and financial system with the global world. While rising global integration has its advantages in terms of expanding the scope and scale of growth of the Indian economy, it also exposes India to global shocks. Hence, maintaining financial stability became an important mandate for the Reserve Bank. This has brought forth the need for effective coordination and consultation with other regulators within the country and abroad.

**Box 2.2: RBI Logo**

The selection of the Bank's common seal to be used as the emblem of the Bank on currency notes, cheques and publications, was an issue that had to be taken up at an early stage of the Bank's formation.

The general ideas on the seal were as follows:

1. The seal should emphasise the Governmental status of the Bank, but not too closely;
2. It should have something Indian in the design;
3. It should be simple, artistic and heraldically correct; and
4. The design should be such that it could be used without substantial alteration for letter heading, etc.

For this purpose, various seals, medals and coins were examined. The East India Company Double Mohur, with the sketch of the Lion and Palm Tree, was found most suitable; however, it was decided to replace the lion by the tiger, the latter being regarded as the more characteristic animal of India!

To meet the immediate requirements in connection with the stamping of the Bank's share certificates, the work was entrusted to a Madras firm. The Board, at its meeting on February 23, 1935, approved the design of the seal but desired improvement of the animal's appearance. Unfortunately it was not possible to make any major changes at that stage. But the Deputy Governor, Sir James Taylor, did not rest content with this. He took keen interest in getting fresh sketches prepared by the Government of India Mint and the Security Printing Press, Nasik. As a basis for good design, he arranged for a photograph to be taken of the statue of the tiger on the entrance gate at Belvedere, Calcutta. Something or the other went wrong with the sketches so that Sir James, writing in September I938, was led to remark: a tree is all right but his tiger looks too like some species of dog, and I am afraid that a design of a dog and a tree would arouse derision among the irreverent...tiger is distinctly good but the tree has spoiled it. The stem is too long and the branches too spidery, but I should have thought that by putting a firm line under the feet of his tiger and making his tree stronger and lower we could get quite a good result from his design. Later, with further efforts, it was possible to have better proofs prepared by the Security Printing Press, Nasik. However, it was eventually decided not to make any change in the existing seal of the Bank, and the new sketches came to be used as an emblem for the Bank's currency notes, letter-heads, cheques and publications issued by the Bank.

Source: *History of the Reserve Bank of India*

The Reserve Bank is the umbrella network for numerous activities, all related to the nation's financial sector, encompassing and extending beyond the functions of a typical central bank.

1. Monetary authority.
2. Issuer of currency.
3. Banker and debt manager to the government.
4. Banker to banks.
5. Regulator of the banking system.
6. Management of foreign exchange.
7. Regulator and supervisor of the payment and settlement systems.
8. Developmental role.

**2.2 Monetary Authority**

Monetary policy refers to the use of instruments under the control of the central bank to regulate the availability, cost and use of money and credit. The goal remains to achieve specific economic objectives like low and stable inflation and promoting growth.

The main objectives of monetary policy in India are:

1. Maintaining price stability.
2. Ensuring adequate flow of credit to the productive sectors of the economy to support economic growth.
3. Financial stability.

The relative emphasis among the objectives varies from time to time, depending on evolving macroeconomic developments. The Reserve Bank's Monetary Policy Department (MPD) formulates monetary policy. The Financial Markets Department (FMD) handles day-to-day liquidity management operations. There are several direct and indirect instruments that are used in the formulation and implementation of monetary policy. The Reserve Bank monitors and conducts analysis of movement of a number of indicators like interest rates, inflation rate, money supply, credit, exchange rate, trade, capital flows and fiscal position, along with trends in output to help in developing policy perspectives.

**2.2.1 Direct Instruments:** Cash reserve ratio (CRR): The share of net demand and time liabilities that banks must maintain as cash balance with the Reserve Bank.

Statutory liquidity ratio (SLR): The share of net demand and time liabilities that banks must maintain in safe and liquid assets, such as, government securities, cash and gold valued at a price not exceeding the current market price.

Refinance facilities: Sector-specific refinance facilities (e.g., against lending to export sector) is provided to banks.

**2.2.2 Indirect Instruments:** Liquidity adjustment facility (LAF): Consists of daily infusion or absorption of liquidity on a repurchase basis, through repo (liquidity injection) and reverse repo (liquidity absorption) auction operations, using government securities as collateral.

Open market operations (OMO): Outright sale/purchase of government securities, in addition to LAF, as a tool to determine the level of liquidity over the medium-term.

**A. Market Stabilisation Scheme (MSS):** This instrument for monetary management was introduced in 2004. Liquidity of a more enduring nature arising from large capital flows is absorbed through sale of short-dated government securities and treasury bills. The mobilised cash is held in a separate government account with the Reserve Bank.

**B. Repo/Reverse Repo Rate:** These rates under the liquidity adjustment facility (LAF) determine the corridor for short-term money market interest rates.

**C. Bank Rate:** It is the rate at which the Reserve Bank is ready to buy or rediscount bills of exchange or other commercial papers.

### 2.3 Issuer of Currency

The Reserve Bank is the nation's sole note issuing authority. Along with the Government of India, RBI is responsible for the design and production and overall management of the nation's currency, with the goal of ensuring an adequate supply of clean and genuine notes. The Reserve Bank also makes sure there is an adequate supply of coins, produced by the government. In consultation with the government, RBI routinely looks into security issues and ways to enhance security features to reduce the risk of counterfeiting or forgery.

Four printing presses actively print notes—Dewas in Madhya Pradesh, Nasik in Maharashtra, Mysore in Karnataka, and Salboni in West Bengal. The presses in Karnataka and West Bengal are set up by BRBNMPL, a wholly-owned subsidiary of the Reserve Bank. The presses in Madhya Pradesh and Maharashtra are owned by the Security Printing and Minting Corporation of India (SPMCIL), a wholly-owned company of the Government of India. Coins are minted by the Government of India. RBI is the agent of the Government for distribution, issue and handling of coins. Four mints are in operation—Mumbai, Noida in Uttar Pradesh, Kolkata, and Hyderabad. RBI's anti-counterfeiting measures include continual upgrades of bank note security features, public awareness campaigns to educate citizens to help prevent circulation of forged or counterfeit notes and installation of note sorting machines.

## 2.4 Banker and Debt Manager to Government

Managing the government's banking transactions is a key role of the RBI. Like individuals, businesses and banks, governments need a banker to carry out their financial transactions in an efficient and effective manner, including the raising of resources from the public. As a banker to the central government, the Reserve Bank maintains its accounts, receives money into and makes payments out of these accounts and facilitates the transfer of government funds.

The role as banker and debt manager to government includes several distinct functions like undertaking banking transactions for the central and state governments to facilitate receipts and payments and maintaining their accounts, managing the governments' domestic debt with the objective of raising the required amount of public debt in a cost-effective and timely manner and developing the market for government securities to enable the government to raise debt at a reasonable cost, provide benchmarks for raising resources by other entities and facilitate transmission of monetary policy actions.

**2.5 Banker to Banks**

Like individual consumers, businesses and organisations of all kinds, banks need their own mechanism to transfer funds and settle inter-bank transactions—such as borrowing from and lending to other Banks—and customer transactions. As the banker to banks, the Reserve Bank fulfils this role. In effect, all banks operating in the country have accounts with the Reserve Bank, just as individuals and businesses have accounts with their respective banks. The Reserve Bank provides similar products and services for the nation's banks to what banks offer their own customers.

As a banker to banks, RBI provides:

Non-interest earning current accounts: Banks hold accounts with the Reserve Bank based on certain terms and conditions, such as maintenance of minimum balances. Banks draw on these accounts to settle their obligations arising from inter-bank settlement systems. Banks can electronically transfer payments to other banks from this account, using the real time gross settlement system (RTGS).

Deposit Account Department: This department helps banks manage their funds position in real time to maintain the optimum balance between surplus and deficit centres.

Remittance facilities: Banks and government departments can use these facilities to transfer funds.

Lender of the last resort: The Reserve Bank provides liquidity to banks unable to raise short-term liquid resources from the inter-bank market.

Like other central banks, the Reserve Bank considers this a critical function because it protects the interests of depositors, which in turn, has a stabilizing impact on the financial system and on the economy as a whole.

Loans and advances: The Reserve Bank provides short-term loans and advances to banks/financial institutions, when necessary, to facilitate lending for specified purposes.

## 2.6 Regulator of the Banking System

The central bank has a critical role to play in ensuring the safety and soundness of the banking system and in maintaining financial stability and public confidence in this system.

As the regulator and supervisor of the banking system, the Reserve Bank protects the interests of depositors, ensures a framework for orderly development and conduct of banking operations conducive to customer interests and maintains overall financial stability through preventive and corrective measures.

As a regulator, the Reserve Bank handles a range of activities, including:

1. Licensing.
2. Prescribing capital requirements.
3. Monitoring governance.
4. Setting prudential regulations to ensure solvency and liquidity of the banks.
5. Prescribing lending to certain priority sectors of the economy.
6. Regulating interest rates in specific areas.
7. Setting appropriate regulatory norms related to income recognition, asset classification, provisioning, investment valuation, exposure limits and the like.
8. Initiating new regulation.

## 2.7 Management of Foreign Exchange

With the transition to a market-based system for determining the external value of the Indian rupee, the foreign exchange market in India gained importance in the early reform period. The Reserve Bank plays a key role in the regulation and development of the foreign exchange market and assumes three broad roles relating to foreign exchange:

1. Regulating transactions related to the external sector and facilitating the development of the foreign exchange market.
2. Ensuring smooth conduct and orderly conditions in the domestic foreign exchange market.
3. Managing the foreign currency assets and gold reserves of the country.

The Reserve Bank is responsible for administration of the Foreign Exchange Management Act, 1999 and regulates the market by issuing licences to Banks and other select institutions to act as Authorised Dealers in foreign exchange. The Foreign Exchange Department (FED) is responsible for the regulation and development of the market. On a given day, the foreign exchange rate reflects the demand for and supply of foreign exchange arising from trade and capital transactions. The RBI's Financial Markets Department (FMD) participates in the foreign exchange market by undertaking sale/purchase of foreign currency to ease volatility in periods of excess demand for/supply of foreign currency. The Department of External Investments and Operations (DEIO) invests the country's foreign exchange reserves built up by purchase of foreign currency from the market.

### 2.8 Regulator/Supervisor of Payment and Settlement Systems

Payment and settlement systems play an important role in improving overall economic efficiency. They consist of all the diverse arrangements that we use to systematically transfer money—currency, paper instruments such as cheques, and various electronic channels. The Reserve Bank has a two-tiered structure. The first tier provides the basic framework for our payment systems. The second tier focuses on supervision of this framework. As part of the basic framework, the Reserve

Bank's network of secure systems handles various types of payment and settlement activities. Here is an overview of the various systems used.

Retail payment systems: Facilitating cheque clearing, electronic funds transfer, through National Electronic Funds Transfer (NEFT), settlement of card payments and bulk payments, such as electronic clearing services.

Large value systems: Facilitating settlement of inter-bank transactions from financial markets. These include:

1. Real Time Gross Settlement System (RTGS): for funds transfers.
2. Securities Settlement System: for the government securities market.
3. Foreign Exchange Clearing: for transactions involving foreign currency.
4. Department of Payment and Settlement Systems: The Reserve Bank's payment and settlement systems regulatory arm.
5. Department of Information Technology: Tech support for the payment systems and for the Reserve Bank's internal IT systems.

## 2.9 Developmental Role

This includes ensuring that credit is available to the productive sectors of the economy, establishing institutions designed to build the country's financial infrastructure, expanding access to affordable financial services and promoting financial education and literacy. Some of the institutions established by the RBI include:

1. Deposit Insurance and Credit Guarantee Corporation (1962), to provide protection to bank depositors and guarantee cover to credit facilities extended to certain categories of small borrowers.
2. Unit Trust of India (1964), the first mutual fund of the country.
3. Industrial Development Bank of India (1964), a

development finance institution for industry.

4. National Bank of Agriculture and Rural Development (1982), for promoting rural and agricultural credit.
5. Discount and Finance House of India (1988), a money market intermediary and a primary dealer in government securities.
6. National Housing Bank (1989), an apex financial institution for promoting and regulating housing finance.
7. Securities and Trading Corporation of India (1994), a primary dealer.

The Reserve Bank continues its developmental role, while specifically focussing on financial inclusion. Key tools in this on-going effort include:

1. Directed credit for lending to priority sector and weaker sections: The goal here is to facilitate/enhance credit flow to employment intensive sectors such as agriculture, micro and small enterprises (MSE), as well as for affordable housing and education loans.
2. Lead Bank Scheme: A commercial bank is designated as a lead bank in each district in the country and this bank is responsible for ensuring banking development in the district through coordinated efforts between banks and government officials.
3. Sector specific refinance: The Reserve Bank makes available refinance to banks against their credit to the export sector.
4. Strengthening and supporting small local banks: This includes regional rural banks and cooperative banks.
5. Financial inclusion: Expanding access to finance for financially excluded people in our country and promoting financial literacy are a part of outreach efforts.

## 2.10 RBI and Customer Service in Banks

RBI has a customer outreach policy which is aimed at informing the public, so that they know what to expect, what choices they have and what rights and obligations they have in relation to banking services. Its customer service initiatives are designed to protect customers' rights, enhance the quality of customer service and strengthen the grievance redressal mechanism in the banking sector as a whole. To facilitate the same, RBI has a customer service department to respond to customer issues. It has also established Banking Codes and Standards Board of India (BCSBI) to encourage transparency in lending and fair pricing. BCSBI aims to provide customers more confidence in the system and encourage more usage of formal banking (www.bcsbi.org.in). RBI has also set up Banking Ombudsman which is quasi-judicial authority for resolving customers' disputes with banks on one hand and between commercial banks, primary cooperative banks and regional rural banks on the other.

### 2.11 Subsidiaries of RBI

The Reserve Bank has the following fully-owned subsidiaries:

**2.11.1 Deposit Insurance and Credit Guarantee Corporation (DICGC):** With a view to integrating the functions of deposit insurance and credit guarantee, the Deposit Insurance Corporation and Credit Guarantee Corporation of India were merged and the present Deposit Insurance and Credit Guarantee Corporation (DICGC) came into existence on July 15, 1978. Deposit Insurance and Credit Guarantee Corporation (DICGC), established under the DICGC Act 1961, is one of the wholly-owned subsidiaries of the Reserve Bank. The DICGC insures all deposits (such as savings, fixed, current, and recurring deposits) with eligible banks, except the following:

1. Deposits of foreign governments.
2. Deposits of Central/State Governments.
3. Inter-bank deposits.
4. Deposits of the State Land Development Banks with the State Cooperative Banks.
5. Any amount due on account of any deposit received

outside India.

6. Any amount, which has been specifically exempted by the corporation with the previous approval of Reserve Bank of India. Every eligible bank depositor is insured up to a maximum of ₹ 1,00,000 (Rupees one lakh) for both principal and interest amount held by him.

**2.11.2 National Housing Bank (NHB):** National Housing Bank was set up on July 9, 1988 under the National Housing Bank Act, 1987 as a wholly-owned subsidiary of the Reserve Bank to act as an apex level institution for housing. NHB has been established to achieve, among other things, the following objectives:

1. To promote a sound, healthy, viable and cost effective housing finance system to all segments of the population and to integrate the housing finance system with the overall financial system.
2. To promote a network of dedicated housing finance institutions to adequately serve various regions and different income groups.
3. To augment resources for the sector and channelize them for housing.
4. To make housing credit more affordable.
5. To regulate the activities of housing finance companies based on regulatory and supervisory authority derived under the Act.
6. To encourage augmentation of supply of buildable land and also building materials for housing and to upgrade the housing stock in the country.
7. To encourage public agencies to emerge as facilitators and suppliers of serviced land for housing.

**2.11.3 Bharatiya Reserve Bank Note Mudran Private Limited (BRBNMPL):** The Reserve Bank established BRBNMPL in February 1995 as a wholly-owned subsidiary to augment the production of bank notes in India and to enable bridging of the gap between supply and demand for Bank notes in the country. The BRBNMPL has been registered as a public limited company under the Companies Act, 1956 with its registered and corporate office situated at Bengaluru. The company manages two presses, one at Mysore in Karnataka and the other at Salboni in West Bengal.

**2.11.4 National Bank for Agriculture and Rural Development (NABARD):** National Bank for Agriculture and Rural Development (NABARD) is one of the subsidiaries where the majority stake is held by the Reserve Bank. NABARD is an apex development bank with a mandate for facilitating credit flow for promotion and development of agriculture, small-scale industries, cottage and village industries, handicrafts and other rural crafts. It also has the mandate to support all other allied economic activities in rural areas, promote integrated and sustainable rural development and secure prosperity of rural areas.

## 2.12 Governors of the Reserve Bank of India

**2.12.1 Sir Osborne Smith:** Sir Osborne Smith was the first Governor of the Reserve Bank. A professional banker, he served for over 20 years with the Bank of New South Wales and 10 years with the Commonwealth Bank of Australia before coming to India in 1926 as a Managing Governor of the Imperial Bank of India. His stewardship of the Imperial Bank won him recognition in banking circles in India. However, his outlook on policy issues like the exchange rates and interest rates was at variance with that of the Government. He resigned prior to the completion of his term of office of three and a half years. Sir Osborne, however, did not sign any bank notes during his tenure.

**2.12.2 Sir James Braid Taylor:** Sir James Braid Taylor was a member of the Indian Civil Service and had served for over a decade in the currency department of the Government of India, initially as a Deputy Controller, later as Controller of the Currency, and thereafter as Additional Secretary in the Finance Department. He was closely associated with the preparation and piloting of the Reserve Bank of India Bill. He served as Deputy Governor of the Bank prior to his appointment as the Governor.

His stewardship saw the Bank through the War years and the financial experiments it engendered and catalysed, including the decisive break away from a silver currency to fiat money. His second term came to an end with his sudden demise.

**2.12.3 Shri Chintaman Dwarkanath Deshmukh:** C.D. Deshmukh, a member of the Indian Civil Service, was the first Indian Governor of the Bank. His association with the Bank commenced in 1939, when he was appointed Government's liaison officer. He later served as Secretary and thereafter in 1941 as Deputy Governor of the Bank. On the demise of James Taylor, he took over stewardship of the Bank and was appointed Governor in August, 1943.

During his tenure as Governor, he represented India at the Bretton Woods negotiations in 1944, saw the transition to Independence and the partition of the country and the division of the assets and liabilities of the Reserve Bank between India and Pakistan. He helped the smooth transition of the Bank from a shareholder's institution to a State-owned organisation, when the Bank was nationalised on 1st January 1949. He later held the office of Union Finance Minister during 1950-56.

**2.12.4 Sir Benegal Rama Rau:** A member of the Indian Civil Service, he was the longest serving Governor of the Bank. Prior to joining the Bank, he served as the Indian Ambassador to the United States.

His tenure witnessed the commencement of the planning era as well innovative initiatives in the spheres of cooperative credit and industrial finance. The recommendations of the All India Rural Credit Survey Committee appointed during his tenure led to the transformation of the Imperial Bank of India to State Bank of India. The proportional reserve system of note issue was replaced by a minimum reserve system to give the Bank greater flexibility. He resigned in the middle of January 1957 before his second extended term of office expired due to differences with the Finance Minister.

**2.12.5 Shri K.G. Ambegaokar:** A member of the Indian Civil Service, he served as Finance Secretary prior to his appointment as Deputy Governor. On the resignation of B. Rama Rau, he was appointed as the interim Governor till H.V.R. Iengar could take over.

He forged closer connections between agricultural enterprise and the Reserve Bank's operations. K.G. Ambegaonkar did not sign any bank notes.

**2.12.6 Shri H.V.R. Iengar:** A member of the Indian Civil Service, he served for a brief while as the Chairman of State Bank of India, before being appointed as the Governor of the Reserve Bank.

His tenure witnessed India's shift to decimal coinage from the earlier system. The period saw conscious efforts to consolidate the Banking industry. The Bank acquired powers in September 1960 to enforce amalgamations and de-licensing of banks. The Bank was also active in catalysing medium-term lending to industry by commercial banks by invoking the concept of refinance which led to the establishment of the Refinance Corporation for Industry Ltd. Deposit insurance for bank deposits was introduced in 1962 making India one of the earliest countries to experiment with deposit insurance. In the sphere of monetary policy, the variable cash reserve ratio was used for the first time as were the selective credit controls.

**2.12.7 Shri P. C. Bhattacharya:** A member of the Indian Audit and Account Service, he served as Secretary in the Finance Ministry and later as Chairman of the State Bank of India prior to his appointment as Governor.

His tenure saw the establishment of the Industrial Development Bank of India (1964), and the establishment of the Agricultural Refinance Corporation (1963) and the Unit Trust of India (1964). Other developments were the introduction of the Credit Authorisation Scheme as an instrument of credit regulation, the devaluation of the Rupee in 1966, with a package of measures including import liberalisation and elimination of export subsidies.

**2.12.8 Shri L.K. Jha:** A member of the Indian Civil Service, he served as Secretary to the Prime Minister, prior to his appointment as Governor.

During his tenure, social controls over commercial banks were introduced as an experiment in 1968, as a part of which a National Credit Council was established. Shortly thereafter, 14 major commercial banks were nationalised in 1969, a step which did not have the endorsement of the Reserve Bank.

Amongst other developments, gold controls were brought on a statutory basis; deposit insurance was in principle extended to cooperative banks; the Lead Bank Scheme was introduced to facilitate credit delivery, and the setting up of the Agricultural Credit Board. L.K. Jha was appointed India's Ambassador to the United States in May 1970 prior to the completion of his term as Governor.

**2.12.9 Shri B.N. Adarkar:** He held the post of Governor during the interregnum till S. Jagannathan could take over as Governor.

He was a professional economist and served for many years in the office of the Economic Adviser of the Government of India and also held important positions in the Ministry of Commerce and Industry prior to his appointment as the Deputy Governor of the Bank.

He also served as India's Executive Director at the IMF and as Deputy Governor, he played an active role in the establishment of the National Institute of Bank Management.

**2.12.10 Shri S. Jagannathan:** He was a member of the Indian Audit and Accounts Service. He had served with the Central Government and thereafter as India's Executive Director at the World Bank, prior to being appointed as the Governor. His tenure of office was characterised by a very active monetary policy in the wake of unprecedented inflation in the country following the oil shock, an exponential expansion of banking offices in pursuance of one of the important objectives of nationalisation; the establishment of

Credit Guarantee Corporation of India, the setting up of State Level Bankers' Committees and the shift to floating rates regime.

He relinquished office to take up the post of the Indian Executive Director at the International Monetary Fund (IMF).

**2.12.11 Shri N.C. Sen Gupta:** He was appointed Governor for three months till K.R. Puri could assume office. Prior to his appointment as the Governor, he was working as Secretary to the Department of Banking of the Ministry of Finance.

**2.12.12 Shri K.R. Puri:** He served as the chairman and managing director of the Life Insurance Corporation of India before his appointment as Governor.

During his tenure, regional rural banks were set up; the Asian Clearing Union commenced operations; the twenty point economic programme was announced and operationalised and a new money supply series introduced.

**2.12.13 Shri M. Narasimham:** He was the first and so far the only Governor to be appointed from the Reserve Bank cadre, having joined the Bank as a research officer in the economic department. He later joined the Government and prior to his appointment as Governor he served as Additional Secretary, Department of Economic Affairs.

He had a short tenure of seven months. He later served as Executive Director for India at the World Bank and thereafter at the IMF after which he served in the Ministry of Finance as Secretary. He was chairperson of the Committee on the Financial System, 1991 and the Committee on Banking Sector Reforms, 1998.

**2.12.14 Dr. I.G. Patel:** An economist and administrator, he joined the Reserve Bank as Governor after serving as Secretary in the Ministry of Finance and thereafter at the UNDP.

His tenure witnessed the demonetization of high denomination notes as well as the 'gold auctions' conducted by the Bank on behalf of Government of India. During his tenure six private sector banks were nationalized, targets for priority sector lending introduced, and the deposit insurance and credit guarantee corporations were merged, and a departmental reorganization was undertaken in the Bank. He played an active role in availing of the IMF's Extended Fund Facility in 1981 due to balance of payments difficulties. This represented the largest arrangement in IMF's history at the time.

**2.12.15 Dr. Manmohan Singh:** An academic and administrator, he had served as Secretary Finance as well as Member Secretary of the Planning Commission prior to his appointment as Governor. During his tenure, comprehensive legal reforms were carried out related to the banking sector and a new chapter introduced in the Reserve Bank of India Act and the urban banks department was set up.

After his tenure in the Bank, he served in various capacities before being appointed Finance Minister. His tenure as Finance Minister was notable for the fact that he heralded in liberalisation and comprehensive reforms in India.

**2.12.16 Shri A. Ghosh:** He was the Deputy Governor of the Bank since 1982 when he was appointed Governor for a brief period of 15 days till R.N. Malhotra could take over. He was earlier the chairman of Allahabad Bank prior to his appointment as the Deputy Governor of the Bank. He was also a Director of the Industrial Development Bank of India and the governing body of the National Institute of Bank Management.

**2.12.17 Shri R.N. Malhotra:** A member of the Indian Administrative Service, he served as Secretary, Finance and Executive Director of the IMF prior to his appointment as Governor.

During his tenure, efforts were made to develop the money markets and new instruments were introduced. The Discount and Finance House of India, the National Housing Bank were set up and the Indira Gandhi Institute of Development Research inaugurated. In the field of rural finance, the service area approach was adopted to catalyse the flow of credit through commercial banks.

**2.12.18 Shri S. Venkitaramanan:** A member of the Indian Administrative Service, he had served as Finance Secretary and adviser to the Government of Karnataka prior to his appointment as Governor.

The country faced difficulties related to the external sector during his tenure. His adroit management saw the country tide over the balance of payments crisis. His term also saw India adopt the IMF's stabilisation programme where the Rupee underwent a devaluation and the launch of the programme of economic reforms.

**2.12.19 Dr. C. Rangarajan:** He was a professional economist. Prior to his appointment as the Governor, he held charge as Deputy Governor for over a decade. He was also a member of the Planning Commission and a member of the Tenth Finance Commission.

His tenure as Governor saw unprecedented central bank activism to put in place a comprehensive set of measures to strengthen and improve the competitive efficiency of the financial sector. New institutions and instruments were introduced and changes in exchange rate management culminated in the establishment of a unified exchange rate. In the field of monetary policy, his tenure saw the historic memorandum signed between the Bank and the Government whereby a cap was put on the automatic finance by the Bank to the Government in the form of ad hoc treasury bills.

**2.12.20 Dr. Bimal Jalan:** He served as Chief Economic Advisor to Government of India, Banking Secretary, Finance Secretary, Member Secretary of Planning Commission, and Chairman of the Economic Advisory Council to the Prime Minister prior to being appointed as Governor. He had also represented India on the Executive Boards of the IMF and the World Bank.

During his tenure, India weathered the Asian Crisis and has seen the consolidation of the gains of liberalization and economic reforms. The monetary policy process was demystified and central Bank communications marked a perceived shift towards transparency.

This period has seen a slew of measures to strengthen the banking sector, establish new institutions and introduce new instruments. The period has been characterized by the strengthening of the balance of payments and forex position, low inflation and soft interest rates.

**Box 2.3 Anecdote of Aspirants, Pensioners and Continuity**

Jobs at the Reserve Bank of India were highly coveted. Just before the Bank opened it doors for business in April 1935, its Calcutta Office advertised fifty odd temporary job vacancies. The response was overwhelming. There were reportedly over ten thousand applications. The journal Indian Finance of March 1935 wrote this rather dramatic report:

"It was not a rain, but a downpour of applicants. They came from all corners of Calcutta-from most mofussil stations of Bengal. The building was chokeful of crowding graduates. The overflow in the streets was so heavy that the traffic was held up; and there was a traffic jam. The men who got into the building could not get out; the crowd in the street, who were all the time pressing towards the entrance of the building, were panting and perspiring; and some fainted in the crush, I understand. The officials who were to make the selection, were nonplussed. Never did any advertisement in Calcutta papers have such pulling power. In sheer desperation, the police were rung up; and their assistance requisitioned to clear up the building and the streets..."

Unfortunately for job aspirants, new recruitments were few. Much of the staff for the Bank's establishment was transferred to it from the Imperial Bank and Government of India. The Government staff were the erstwhile employees of the Office of the Controller of the Currency from whom the Bank took over the function of Currency Management and issuance of Public Debt.

In the late 1980s, a special cell was set up in the Department of Expenditure and Budgetary Control (DEBC) to look into the accounts of the 'Government Transferred Pensioners'.

Contd...

While doing so one of the records that came to light was that of Abdool Osman, a Duftary and resident of Sadinagar Village, Manikgunj, District of Dacca then in undivided India. Shri Abdool had joined Government of India service on 4th June, 1885 and retired from the Bank in March, 1939 at the age of 75 after a service span of 51 years and 29 days with seven extensions of service to his credit. His 'Last Pay Certificate' indicated a salary of Rs. 27 per month which he had been drawing for over sixteen years without any annual increment. Apparently, Abdool Osman retired a contented man with a pension of Rs. 8 to look forward to every month!

Duftary-literally 'office keeper' was a term applied to 'inferior staff,' as they were then known. Their job was to store, retrieve and maintain office files. While this job has been largely taken over by computers, the term is still in vogue and the post still exists.

**2.12.21 Dr. Yaga Venugopal Reddy:** The twenty-first Governor, was a member of the Indian Administrative Service. He spent most of his career in the areas of finance and planning. He served as Secretary (Banking) in Ministry of Finance, Additional Secretary, Ministry of Commerce, Joint Secretary in Ministry of Finance in Government of India, Principal Secretary, Government of Andhra Pradesh and had a six year tenure as Deputy Governor of the Reserve Bank of India. Prior to his appointment as the Governor, Dr. Reddy was India's Executive Director on the Board of the International Monetary Fund.

Dr. Reddy has made significant policy contributions in the areas of financial sector reforms; trade finance; monitoring of balance of payments and exchange rate; external commercial borrowings; centre-state financial relations; regional planning; and public enterprise reform and has been closely associated with institution building. He has several publications to his credit mainly in areas relating to finance, planning and public enterprises.

**2.12.22 Dr. D. Subbarao:** The 22$^{nd}$ and the present Governor of the Reserve Bank of India, was a member of the Indian Administrative Service. Before joining the Reserve

Bank in 2008, he served as Finance Secretary, Ministry of Finance, Government of India.

Dr. Subbarao was a topper in the All India Civil Service examination for entry into Indian Administrative Services and Indian Foreign Services in 1972. He was one of the first IITians to join the civil services.

# 3

# State Bank of India (SBI)

State Bank of India (SBI) is the country's largest commercial bank. The government-controlled bank (the Indian government maintains a stake of 59.40 percent in SBI) also operates the world's largest branch network, with 13,542 branch offices throughout India and staffed by 2,22,933 employees as on 31st March 2011. SBI is also present worldwide, with seven international subsidiaries in the United States, Canada, Nepal, Bhutan, Nigeria, Mauritius, and the United Kingdom, and 156 branch offices in 32 countries.

## 3.1 Evolution of SBI

The evolution of State Bank of India can be traced back to the first decade of the 19th century. A plan for a semi-government bank was formulated in 1801 for stabilizing rates of interest and mobilizing credit. And so was born the Bank of Calcutta on 2nd June 1806 hedged in a house at 8, Post Office Street, Calcutta at a monthly rent of ₹ 300.When the court of directors granted it a charter and re-designated it as the Bank of Bengal, it became the first joint-stock bank in British India. The bank was redesignated as the Bank of Bengal, three years later, on 2nd January 1809. It was the first ever joint-stock bank of British India, established under the sponsorship of the Government of Bengal. Subsequently, the Bank of Bombay (established on 15th April 1840) and the Bank of Madras (established on 1st July 1843) followed the Bank of Bengal.

All these banks were founded at the initiative of the British in the three presidencies into which the East India Company had divided their sphere of operations in India. The banks of Bengal, Bombay and Madras were primarily Anglo-Indian creations and were brought into existence through the initiatives of British officials and businessmen living in India. They derived their ideas from their experience in India and from the general feedback and experience in Britain about Banks and other economic institutions and their relations with the government. These three banks remained at the apex of modern banking in India till their amalgamation as the Imperial Bank of India on 27th January 1921.

The three Presidency banks came into existence either as a result of the compulsions of imperial finance or by the felt needs of local European commerce and were not imposed from outside in an arbitrary manner to modernise India's economy. Their evolution was, however, shaped by ideas culled from similar developments in Europe and England, and was influenced by changes occurring in the structure of both the local trading environment and those in the relations of the Indian economy to the economy of Europe and the global economic framework.

The establishment of the Bank of Bengal marked the advent of limited liability, joint-stock banking in India. So was the associated innovation in banking, viz. the decision to allow the Bank of Bengal to issue notes, which would be accepted for payment of public revenues within a restricted geographical area. This right of note issue was very valuable not only for the Bank of Bengal but also its two siblings, the Banks of Bombay and Madras. It meant an accretion to the capital of the banks, a capital on which the proprietors did not have to pay any interest. The concept of deposit banking was also an innovation because the practice of accepting money for safekeeping (and in some cases, even investment on behalf of the clients) by the indigenous bankers had not spread as a general habit in most parts of India. But, for a long time, and especially up to the time that the three presidency banks had a right of note issue, bank notes and government balances made up the bulk of the investible resources of the banks.

Bank of Bengal Head Office

Bank of Madras Head Office

Bank of Bombay Head Office

The three banks were governed by royal charters, which were revised from time to time. Each charter provided for a share capital, four-fifth of which was privately subscribed and the rest owned by the provincial government. The members of the board of directors, which managed the affairs of each bank, were mostly proprietary directors representing the large European managing agency houses in India. The rest were government nominees, invariably civil servants, one of whom was elected as the president of the board.

A major change in the conditions of operation of the Banks of Bengal, Bombay and Madras occurred after 1860. With the passing of the Paper Currency Act of 1861, the right of note issue of the presidency banks was abolished and the Government of India assumed from 1 March 1862 the sole power of issuing paper currency within British India. The task of management and circulation of the new currency notes was conferred on the presidency banks and the Government undertook to transfer the treasury balances to the banks at places where the banks would open branches. None of the three banks had till then any branches (except the sole attempt and that too a short-lived one by the Bank of Bengal at Mirzapore in 1839) although the charters had given them such authority. But as soon as the three presidency banks were assured of the free use of government treasury balances at places where they would open branches, they embarked on branch expansion at a rapid pace.

By 1876, the branches, agencies and sub-agencies of the three presidency banks covered most of the major parts and many of the inland trade centres in India. While the Bank of Bengal had eighteen branches including its head office, seasonal branches and sub-agencies, the Banks of Bombay and Madras had fifteen each.

These three banks dominated the modern banking scenario in India, until when they were amalgamated along with their 70 branches to form the Imperial Bank of India, on 27th January 1921.The triad had been transformed into a monolith and a giant among Indian commercial banks had emerged. The Imperial Bank during the three and a half decades of its existence recorded an impressive growth in terms of offices, reserves, deposits, investments and advances, the increases in some cases amounting to more than six-fold. The financial status and security inherited from its forerunners no doubt provided a firm and durable platform. But the lofty traditions of banking which the Imperial Bank consistently maintained and the high standard of integrity it observed in its operations inspired confidence in its depositors that no other bank in India could perhaps then equal. All these enabled the Imperial Bank to acquire a pre-eminent position in the Indian banking industry and also secure a vital place in the country's economic life.

State Bank of India was created on 1st July 1935. But this creation was preceded by years of deliberations on the need for a 'State Bank of India'. What eventually emerged was a 'half-way house' combining the functions of a commercial bank and a quasi-central bank. The establishment of the Reserve Bank of India as the central bank of the country in 1935 ended the quasi-central banking role of the Imperial Bank. The latter ceased to be bankers to the Government of India and instead became agent of the Reserve Bank for the transaction of government business at centres at which the central bank was not established. But it continued to maintain currency chests and small coin depots and operate the remittance facilities scheme for other banks and the public on terms stipulated by the Reserve Bank. It also acted as a bankers' bank by holding their surplus cash and granting them advances against authorized securities. The management of the bank clearing houses also continued with it at many places where the Reserve Bank did not have offices. The bank was also the biggest tenderer at the treasury bill auctions conducted by the Reserve Bank on behalf of the Government.

The establishment of the Reserve Bank simultaneously saw important amendments being made to the constitution of the Imperial Bank converting it into a purely commercial bank. The earlier restrictions on its business were removed and the bank was permitted to undertake foreign exchange business and executor and trustee business for the first time. When India attained freedom, the Imperial Bank had a capital base (including reserves) of ₹ 11.85 crore, deposits and advances of ₹ 275.14 crore and ₹ 72.94 crore respectively and a network of 172 branches and more than 200 sub-offices extending all over the country.

An important turning point in the history of State Bank of India was the launch of the First Five Year Plan of independent India, in 1951. The Plan aimed at serving the Indian economy in general and the rural sector of the country, in particular. Until the Plan, the commercial banks of the country, including the Imperial Bank of India, confined their services to the urban sector. Moreover, they were not equipped to respond to the growing needs of the economic revival taking shape in the rural areas of the country. Therefore, in order to serve the economy as a whole and rural sector in particular, the All India Rural Credit Survey Committee recommended the formation of a state-partnered and state-sponsored bank.

The All India Rural Credit Survey Committee proposed the take-over of the Imperial Bank of India, and integrating with it, the former state-owned or state-associate banks. Subsequently, an Act was passed in the Parliament of India in May 1955. As a result, the State Bank of India (SBI) was established on 1st July 1955. As per Chapter III of The State Bank of India Act, 1955 relating to "transfer of undertaking of The Imperial Bank to State Bank", (i) subject to the other provisions contained in this Act, on the appointed day, (a) all shares in the capital of the Imperial Bank shall be transferred to, and shall vest in, the Reserve Bank, free of all trusts, liabilities and encumbrances, and (b) the undertaking of the Imperial Bank shall be transferred to, and shall vest in, the State Bank. Thus, all shares in the capital of the Imperial Bank of India were vested in the RBI. The new bank took on the triple role of a commercial bank, a banker's bank and a banker to the government. SBI was registered with an authorised capital of ₹ 20 crore, and an issued and paid up capital of ₹ 5,62,50,000 divided into 562,500 shares of ₹ 100 each. Every person who on the 30th June, 1955, was registered as a holder of shares in the Imperial Bank of India was paid by the Reserve Bank of India. This resulted in making the State Bank of India more powerful, because as much as a quarter of the resources of the Indian banking system were controlled directly by the State.

The State Bank of India emerged as a pacesetter, with its operations carried out by the 480 offices comprising branches, sub-offices and three local head offices, inherited from the Imperial Bank. Instead of serving as mere repositories of the community's savings and lending to creditworthy parties, the State Bank of India catered to the needs of the customers, by banking purposefully. The bank served the heterogeneous financial needs of the planned economic development. On 10th September 1959 State Bank of India (Subsidiary Bank) Act was passed. On 1st October 1959, State Bank of Hyderabad became the first subsidiary of SBI. During this period, State Bank of Jaipur, State Bank of Bikaner, State Bank of Indore, State Bank of Travancore, State Bank of Mysore, State Bank Patiala and State Bank of Saurashtra became subsidiaries of the Bank. The Bhor State Bank Ltd. was amalgamated with the Bank to bring the total number of minor state associated banks so amalgamated to five. A scheme for amalgamation of the Bank of Aundh Ltd. was also approved. On 20th August, 1962 the Unit Bank Ltd. Chennai was taken over by the Bank.

In October 1963, a branch in London became bankers to the Indian High Commission, thereby taking over a function till then performed by the office of RBI. Of the other business transacted by the branch, an important aspect was medium term loans mostly to Indian shipping companies. On 8th November, 1969, the Bank of Behar Ltd. was amalgamated. With effect from 26th August, 1985 the Bank of Cochin Ltd.

with 108 branches was also amalgamated with the Bank. In 1986, on 1st August, a new subsidiary named SBI Capital Market Ltd. functioning independently, and took up leasing business and certain other new services. Up to the end of the year 1987, the Bank had sponsored 30 regional rural banks (RRBs) covering 66 backward and under-banked districts in the country. During February 1991, the bank set up a new subsidiary called the SBI Factors and Commercial Services Pvt. Ltd. for rendering factoring services to the industrial and commercial units in Western India. In 1992, the bank sponsored 30 RRBs with a network of 3189 offices covering 102 backward and under-banked districts of the country.

Today, the State Bank of India is the country's oldest financial institution with a strong balance sheet size, number of branches, market capital and profit figures. It has undergone a transformation to keep up with the changing times. It has forayed into several new segments including strategic tie-ups for pension funds, general insurance, custodial services, private equity, mobile banking, POS merchant acquisition, advisory services, a slew of new structured products, etc.

Some of the other long-term goals of the bank include expansion of its rural banking base to cover 100,000 villages. On the other end of the scale, it is also looking to grow mid-sized to large corporates by providing access to a slew of innovative products and services. The only Indian bank to get featured in the Fortune 500 list, the Bank today has 13542 branches with staff strength of 2,22,933 as on 31st March 2011 and is well positioned to be the bank of the masses and has the largest banking network to offer to the Indian customer.

The bank is forging ahead with cutting edge technology and innovative new banking models, to expand its rural banking base, looking at the vast untapped potential. It is also focusing at the top end of the market, on wholesale banking capabilities to provide India's growing mid/large corporates with a complete array of products and services. It is consolidating its global treasury operations and entering into structured products and derivative instruments. Today, the bank is the largest provider of infrastructure debt and the largest arranger of external commercial borrowings in the country.

**3.2 Awards Won by SBI**

State Bank of India has won many awards including the IDRBT Banking Technology Excellence Award 2011 in Mobile Banking category, the PC Quest "Best IT Implementation Award 2010", for its project "Green IT@SBI", "CNBC Awaaz Award 2010" for most preferred bank for home loans, credit cards and "Most Credible Bank, IDRBT Banking Technology Excellence Award 2009" for best mobile banking and payment application and best use of technology for financial inclusion, the prestigious international award "Innovation in Banking Technology Award 2010" instituted by The Banker Magazine, London, for its project on Green ATM Installation, "The Asian Banker Achievement Award" Singapore, 2010 for the strongest bank in India.

State Bank of India was the eventual winner for the "Innovation in Eco-IT" category in which JP Morgan, Investment Bank, USA and Itau Unibanco, Brazil were in the final reckoning with SBI. In electronic payment category; State Bank of India was adjudged the Best Bank 2009 by Business India (August, 2009); Most Admired Infrastructure Financier Award by KPMG; Top Public Sector Bank under SME Financing by Dun and Bradstreet; Voted for the third year in a row as the most preferred housing loan and most preferred bank in the CNBC AWAAZ Consumer Awards in a survey conducted by CNBC TV18 in association with AG Nielsen & Company; Awarded the best home loan provider as well as the best bank by Outlook Money Awards, 2008; Improved its ranking in Fortune 500 Global List, "Forbes" list of 2000 largest companies in the world; "Banker" list of top 1000 world banks; Brand Finance–Global 500 Financial Brand recognition, to name a few.

### 3.3 Corporate Social Responsibility (CSR)

CSR philosophy of the bank:

1. Bank is a corporate citizen, with resources at its command and benefits which it derives from operating in society in general. It, therefore, owes a solemn duty to the less fortunate and underprivileged members of the same society.
2. Staff members are encouraged to make their contribution by understanding the aspirations of the public around them and by endeavouring to evolve measures to remove indisputable social and developmental lacunae. This will lead to their self-development and improvement of the bank's image besides development of the community.

The bank was awarded Reader's Digest Pegasus Corporate Social Responsibility Award, 2007 in recognition of its contribution towards rural community development.

As of March 2011, it had assets of US$ 370 billion with over 13,500 branches including 150 overseas branches globally. In 2008, the government took over the stake held by the Reserve Bank of India. SBI is ranked No. 292 globally in Fortune Global 500 list in 2011. The Bank provides a range of banking products through its vast network of branches in India and overseas, including products aimed at non-resident Indians (NRIs). The State Bank Group, with over 16,000 branches, has the largest Banking branch network in India. It has 14 local head offices situated at Chandigarh, Delhi, Lucknow, Patna, Kolkata, Guwahati (North-East Circle), Bhubaneswar, Hyderabad, Chennai, Trivandram, Bengaluru, Mumbai, Bhopal and Ahmedabad and 57 zonal offices that are located at important cities throughout the country. Today, SBI is a regional banking behemoth and is one of the largest financial institutions in the world. State Bank of India is the 29th most reputed company in the world according to Forbes. SBI is also the only bank featured in the coveted "Top 10 brands of India" list in an annual survey conducted by Brand Finance and The Economic Times in 2010.

SBI is looking to go on an expansion spree in India as well as in the international arena. SBI is currently undertaking the task of raising sufficient capital for growth and consolidation.

### 3.4 Associates of SBI

The State Bank Group with a network of 18,266 branches including 4,724 branches of its five associate banks, dominates the banking industry in India.

In addition to banking, the Group, through its various subsidiaries, provides a whole range of financial services, which include life insurance, general insurance, merchant banking, mutual funds, credit card, factoring, security trading, pension fund management and primary dealership in the money market. SBI's five Associate Banks had a market share of 5.88 percent in deposits and 6.00 percent in advances as on last Friday of March 2011. State Bank of Indore, one of the associate banks, was acquired on 26th August 2010 after the final approval from RBI and GoI. State Bank of Saurastra had been merged with State Bank of India on 13th September, 2008.

**3.4.1 SBI Capital Markets Ltd. (SBICAP):** SBICAP undertakes merchant banking activities, advisory services, project appraisal, credit syndication and securities broking. SBICAP's current focus is on infrastructure project advisory and syndication mandates, particularly in sectors, such as, urban infrastructure and power, which are reckoned as the growth drivers.

The other focus areas are public issues of equity, book-building issues, debt placements, broking, and sales and distribution. SBICAP is a leader in India in project finance with over 40 percent market share.

SBICAPs has forged ahead in issue management, project advisory and structured finance, sales and distribution. It focused on infrastructure project advisory and syndication mandates, particularly in the energy sector, which is reckoned as the critical growth driver in the growth of the economy.

On the international front, SBICAPs bagged an infrastructure (water) advisory assignment from the Ministry of National Economy, Oman and was an integral part of the team effort for SBI's first acquisition of a bank overseas. It was also associated with SBI for providing advisory in respect of participation of Societe Generale Asset Management, France in SBI Mutual Funds.

The following are some of the many awards/recognitions won by the Company:

1. Bank of the year award 2010 for Asia-Pacific Region for the 3rd consecutive year by Thomson Reuters.
2. Loan House of the Year Award for the 2nd consecutive year by IFR Asia.
3. Ranked No. 1 Global Mandated Lead Arrangers for 2010 by PFI (Thomson Reuters) for the second successive year.
4. Ranked No. 1 Global Lead Arrangers for the second successive year by Dealogic.
5. Ranked 1st with an impressive market share of 13.3 percent for the 1st quarter of calendar 2011 on the Asia Ex-Japan Syndicated Loans Table as per Bloomberg.
6. Ranked 2nd in terms of issues handled and 3rd in terms of amount raised during the financial year 2010-11.
7. Ranked 1st in Rights Issues-both in terms of number of issues and amount raised.
8. Ranked 1st in number of PSU divestment issues.

The company has posted PAT of ₹ 374.72 crore as on 31st March 2011 as against ₹ 137.12 crore as on 31st March 2010 thus recording YoY growth of 173 percent. The Company also declared an interim dividend of 400 percent.

**3.4.2 SBICAP Securities Limited (SSL):** SSL, a wholly-owned subsidiary of SBI Capital Markets Ltd., besides offering equity broking services to retail and institutional clients both in cash as well as in futures and options segments, is also engaged in sales and distribution of other financial products like mutual funds, etc. SSL has 100 branches and offers demat, e-broking, e-IPO and e-MF services to both retail and institutional clients. SSL currently has more than 1.89 lakh customers in their books. The Company has posted a profit of ₹ 4.59 crore as on 31st March 2011.

**3.4.3 SBI Funds Management Pvt. Ltd. (SBI Funds):** SBI Funds is the asset management company (AMC) set up for managing the affairs of SBI Mutual Fund. SBIFMPL, the mutual fund arm of SBI, is the 6th largest fund house in terms of assets under management and a leading player in the market with over 6 million investors.

The schemes of the fund house have performed consistently over the years and have emerged as the preferred investment for investors. The company posted a PAT of ₹ 78.85 crore as on 31st March 2011 registering a YoY growth of 4 percent.

The average assets under management (AUM) of the company stood at ₹ 41,672 crore in March 2011 as against ₹ 37,417 crore as on March 2010 achieving a YoY growth of 11 percent as against the growth of 6 percent for the mutual fund industry.

**3.4.4 SBI DFHI Ltd. (SBI DFHI):** SBI acquired Asian Development Bank's and Industrial Investment Bank of India's stake (4.69 percent and 0.47 percent respectively) in SBI DFHI. SBI group holds 72.17 percent share in the company, which is a primary dealer.

The Institution was created by RBI to support the book building process in primary auctions of Government securities and provides necessary depth and liquidity to the secondary market in government securities. SBI DFHI Ltd. was created out of the merger in 2004 of two leading players in the domestic money and debt markets, the RBI promoted Discount and Finance House of India (DFHI) and SBI Gilts Ltd.

It is a market leader in the primary dealer segment of the domestic debt market. For the period ended 31st March 2011, the Company's PAT was ₹ 56.94 crore as against ₹ 89.23 crore as on 31st March 2010. The market share of SBIDFHI has increased from 2.71 percent as on 31st March 2010 to 3.41

percent as on 31st March 2011.The secondary market turnover during the year was ₹ 97,885 crore as against ₹ 78,911 crore during the corresponding period in 2010 (YoY growth of 24 percent).

**3.4.5 SBI Cards and Payments Services Pvt. Ltd. (SBICPSL):** SBI Cards, the only stand-alone credit card issuing company in India, is a joint venture between State Bank of India and GE Capital Corporation, wherein SBI holds 60 percent stake. The "Cards in Force" (CIF) of the Company stands at 23 lakh and the receivables are at ₹ 1,795 crore at the end of March 2011. The company has posted a net profit of ₹ 7.10 crore as on March 2011 as against a loss of ₹ 152.4 crore as on 31st March 2010. SBI Card has emerged as the most trusted brand by being the undisputed Gold Award winner in Reader's Digest Trusted Brands Survey 2010 for the third year in a row.

**3.4.6 SBI Commercial and International Bank Ltd. (SBICI):** As at the end of March 2011, the aggregate deposits and total advances of SBICI stood at ₹ 453.27 crore and ₹ 271.43 crore respectively. The bank recorded an operating and net profit of ₹ 5.25 crore and ₹ 4.21 crore respectively. The net NPA as at the end of March 2011 was NIL.

**3.4.7 SBICAPS Ventures Limited (SVL):** SVL is a wholly-owned subsidiary of SBI Capital Markets Ltd. SVL earned a net profit of ₹ 0.59 crore during 2010-11. SVL sold its stake in SS Ventures Services Ltd., a venture capital fund set up jointly by SVL and SBI Holdings Inc (Softbank), Japan and its stake in India Japan Fund to SBI Holdings Inc. and Knowledge Investments (Mauritius) Ltd. at a total consideration of ₹ 3.47 crore and ₹ 2.60 lakh respectively.

**3.4.8 SBICAP (UK) Ltd. (SUL):** SUL is a wholly-owned subsidiary of SBI Capital Markets Ltd. SUL has booked a revenue of ₹ 2.16 crore and has posted a net profit of ₹ 0.20 crore despite the global recessionary scenario. SUL is positioning itself as a relationship outfit for SBI Capital Markets in UK and Europe. Relationships are being built with

FIIs, financial institutions, law firms, accounting firms, etc. to market the business products of SBICAP.

**3.4.9 SBICAP Trustee Co. Ltd. (STCL):** SBICAP Trustee Co. Ltd. (STCL), a wholly-owned subsidiary of SBI Capital Markets Ltd., which commenced security trustee business with effect from 1st August 2008 earned a gross income of ₹ 8.31 crore and a net profit of ₹ 4.43 crore during 2010-11 as against gross income of ₹ 3.78 crore and net profit of ₹ 1.94 crore during 2009-10.

**3.4.10 SBI Global Factors Ltd. (SBIGFL):** SBIGFL is one of the leading factoring companies in India which has the highest market share (over 90 percent) in export and import factoring. During the year ended 31st March 2011, the turnover of the company decreased to ₹ 7,605 crore from ₹ 12,978 crore as on 31st March 2010 due to the sluggish growth in industrial production during the year impacting the top line growth.

The company incurred a loss of ₹ 125.62 crore during the year ended 31st March 2011 as against a profit of ₹ 6.58 crore earned on 31st March 2010 mainly on account of slow down in economy and due to higher provisioning for NPAs and write-offs.

**3.4.11 SBI Factors and Commercial Services Pvt. Ltd (SBI Factors):** SBI Factors, a subsidiary of State Bank of India (SBI) is one of the leading factoring companies in India with an asset base of ₹ 700.10 crore as on September 30, 2005. It was established in February 1991 with the primary objective to provide domestic factoring services to small and medium enterprises (SMEs). Factoring is a collection and finance service designed to improve the cash flow position of SMEs by turning their credit invoices into ready cash. The major strength of the company is that it has put in place a technology driven platform for offering integrated receivables management. SBI and its associate banks hold 70 percent stake in SBI Factors. SBIF offers domestic factoring with recourse and without recourse, purchase bill factoring, factoring of usance bills under LC, channel financing of dealers/distributors and export factoring facilities. All its products have been well received by its clients.

**3.4.12 SBI Life Insurance Company Ltd (SBI LIFE):** SBI Life Insurance, India's largest private life insurance, is a joint venture between State Bank of India and BNP Paribas Assurance. SBI owns 74 percent of the total capital and BNP Paribas Assurance the remaining 26 percent. SBI Life Insurance has an authorized capital of ₹ 2,000 crore and a paid up capital of ₹ 1,000 crore.

BNP Paribas Assurance is the insurance arm of BNP Paribas-Euro Zone's leading Bank. BNP Paribas, part of the world's top 10 groups of banks by market value and part of Europe's top 3 banking companies, is one of the oldest foreign banks with a presence in India dating back to 1860.

BNP Paribas Assurance is the fourth largest life insurance company in France, and a worldwide leader in creditor insurance products offering protection to over 50 million clients. BNP Paribas Assurance operates in 41 countries mainly through the bank assurance and partnership model.

SBI Life has a unique multi-distribution model comprising bank assurance, retail agency and institutional alliances and group corporate channels for distribution of insurance products. Gross premium of the company crossed ₹ 12,000 crore with YoY growth of 28 percent. SBI Life has a market share of 19.22 percent of the total market share of private insurers which stood at31.30 percent as on March 31, 2011.

Overall market share (including Life Insurance Corporation of India) of SBI Life stood at 6.02 percent as at March 31, 2011. The company recorded a PAT of ₹ 366.30 crore as on March 31, 2011as against ₹ 276.46 crore as on March 31, 2010. The assets under management of SBI Life recorded a growth of 40 percent YoY to reach ₹ 40,162 crore as on 31st March 2011. The total number of branches of SBI Life is 629. ICRA has reaffirmed IAAA rating to the company indicating highest claim paying ability. CRISIL has reaffirmed its highest financial rating AAA—Stable.

The following are some of the awards/recognitions achieved by the company during 2010-11:

1. NDTV Profit business leadership 2010-11 award for organizational excellence.
2. Bloomberg UTV Award for financial excellence, 2010-11.
3. Outlook Money Award Runner Up for the best life insurance company, 2010-11.
4. ICS quality champion award, 2010-11.

SBI Life Insurance's mission is to emerge as the leading company offering a comprehensive range of life insurance and pension products at competitive prices, ensuring high standards of customer service and world class operating efficiency.

SBI Life has a unique multi-distribution model encompassing bank assurance, agency and corporate solutions. SBI Life extensively leverages the SBI Group relationship as a platform for cross-selling insurance products along with its numerous banking product packages such as housing loans and personal loans. Agency channel, comprising of the most productive force of over 68,000 insurance advisors, offers door to door insurance solutions to customers.

**3.4.13 SBI General Insurance Company Limited:** SBI General Insurance Company Limited is a joint venture between the State Bank of India and Insurance Australia Group (IAG). SBI owns 74 percent of the total capital and IAG the remaining 26 percent. SBI General commenced its business operations in India in March 2010 in a limited way and is working towards a nationwide launch with a larger product portfolio.

SBI General is a technology driven company with state-of-the-art IT systems. It is a multi-product, multi-segment and multi-channel company. SBI General is in the process of setting up a unique multi-distribution model encompassing bank assurance, agency, broking and retail direct (on-line and tele sales) channels. SBI General's vision is to emerge as the most trusted protection provider with fair and transparent business practices and lead the nation's effort in increasing general insurance penetration as well as partnering the nation in reducing risks systematically.

**3.4.14 SBI-SG Global Securities Services Private Limited:** SBI-SG Global Securities Services Private Limited is a joint venture between State Bank of India (SBI) and Society Generale Securities Services (SGSS). This joint venture has been set up to offer high quality custody services, fund accounting and fund administration, risk analysis and performance measurement and registrar and transfer agency services to domestic investors like financial institutions, mutual funds, insurance companies, pension funds, portfolio management services, private banks, corporates, brokers and overseas investors like global custodians or foreign institutional investors in the Indian securities market.

The joint venture is leveraging SBI's strength in the Indian financial sector and SGSS is contributing its recognized experience and best practices as one of the leading global custodians providing securities services across 80 countries world-wide. It has a state-of-the-art service delivery with total focus on rendering world class service to all the major players in the Securities Industry in India.

**3.4.15 SBI Pension Funds Pvt. Ltd. (SBIPF):** SBIPF is one of the three fund managers appointed by Pension Fund Regulatory and Development Authority (PFRDA) for management of pension funds under the new pension system for Central Government (except Armed Forces) and State Government Employees. SBIPF, a wholly-owned subsidiary of the State Bank Group, commenced its operations from April 2008. The total assets under management of the company as on March 31, 2011 were ₹ 3,764.11 crore (YoY growth of 65 percent). As at 31st March 2011, SBIPF was managing 44 percent of the corpus under the Central government scheme, 39 percent under State government schemes and 64 percent under the informal sector. The company recorded a net profit of ₹ 0.32 lakh as on March 31, 2011.

# 4

# Subsidiaries of State Bank of India

The integration of the banking system of the princely states merging into the Indian Union acquired importance soon after Independence. Several of these states had banks associated with them which discharged important banking and treasury responsibilities on their behalf. Many of the other banks were important and were the most significant local banking institutions in the areas where they operated. The diversity of circumstance, forms of ownership and organization, relations and functional arrangements between governments of the princely states and their associated banks varied widely. Some of the former princely state owned banks which they ran as government departments, while others owned a major portion of the share capital in their 'state' banks. In a few cases, state-associated banks were almost entirely privately-owned and, in one case-that of the Krishna Ram Baldeo Bank, Gwalior—by the ruler himself. Some states had banking arrangements with commercial banks and conducted treasury work, either wholly or partly, through government departments.

Diversity also marked the constitution of these enterprises. Some state banks were constituted by acts passed or promulgated locally while the Bank of Baroda, notably, was incorporated under the Companies Act of the Baroda State. At the other extreme, the Bank of Patiala was set up by a firman of the ruler while the Sri Ram Chandra Laxman Bank, Dungarpur, which too did not have a written constitution, was probably set up on the basis of a verbal order of the ruler. There were about fifty-four state-owned or controlled banks (hereafter referred to as state banks or state-associated banks) of various sizes in March 1952. In the changed political conditions, governments of states as they were constituted in independent India came to inherit the interests which the former princely states held in these institutions. State banks varied enormously in size, with the Bank of Baroda which was the largest of them—all having, for instance, deposits running into several crores of rupees. At the other extreme, the aggregate deposits of the Bank of Barwani amounted to a princely sum of ₹ 3,000.

After 1950, it became possible to distinguish two categories of state banks. The first category comprised institutions whose governmental responsibilities largely fell into disuse following the amalgamation of the states of which they were bankers with existing or new states of the Union. A relatively large number of smaller state banks in this category were weak and were on the verge of liquidation. Securing the orderly winding-up of their affairs or amalgamating them with stronger banks became an important focus of the bank's efforts in relation to these institutions. The second category comprised the larger state banks. These banks had a major presence in their respective states particularly in the non urban areas and they also continued to discharge some governmental banking functions even under the new political arrangement.

The Reserve Bank's counsel had already been sought by the Saurashtra government in 1949 for reorganizing banks associated with the princely states of Saurashtra. At the bank's instance, the Bhavnagar Darbar Bank was constituted as the State Bank of Saurashtra and three other former state banks in the state merged with it. The new bank came into existence early in 1950. At a later stage, steps were taken to merge two more minor state banks with the State Bank of Saurashtra. The Reserve Bank recognized that the former state banks represented an 'important link in the chain of Indian banking' which could not afford to remain unregulated for long.

The Law Ministry in the Government of India suggested a 'simple enactment 'to authorize the bank to examine the constitution and financial position of each state bank in order to determine its future. The policy to persuade state-associated banks to voluntarily bring themselves under the purview of the Banking Companies Act was quite successful and by the end of March 1952, twenty-nine of the fifty-four state-associated banks had come with in the scope of this Act. The remaining sixteen banks, which included some of the larger state-associated banks such as the Bank of Patiala, the Hyderabad State Bank, the State Bank of Saurashtra, the Mayurbhanj State Bank, and the Bank of Baghelkhand, could not be brought under the Banking Companies Act without amendments to their constitutions.

The Rural Banking Enquiry Committee found that while the Imperial Bank of India carried out some treasury and banking functions for governments of the different states, the latter had entrusted a major part of these functions tone or more local banking institutions. Among these were the newly-formed State Bank of Saurashtra, and to some extent, the Central Bank of India in Saurashtra, and the Bank of Mysore in Mysore State. In Rajasthan, the Imperial Bank of India, the State Bank of Bikaner, the Bank of Jaipur, and the Bank of Rajasthan shared the banking and treasury business of the state government.

In Hyderabad, the Hyderabad State Bank was entrusted with treasury and banking work, as also that related to the management of public debt and currency, while the Imperial Bank of India too fulfilled a limited set of treasury functions. In Travancore-Cochin, the Imperial Bank of India did the central government's treasury work at Trivandrum, while the state government's cash work was undertaken by the Central Bank of India at Ernakulam. The remaining treasury work was done departmentally by the state government which also had remittance arrangements with some Banks. In Patiala and East Punjab States Union (PEPSU), the Bank of Patiala and the Imperial Bank of India managed the banking work. The state government also maintained accounts with other banks both in the state and outside.

In Madhya Bharat, on the other hand, the bulk of the government work was undertaken by the Bank of Indore, with the Imperial Bank of India playing little or no role in the arrangements. Placing the recommendations of the Rural Banking Enquiry Committee before the Central Board in December 1951, the Governor, B. Rama Rau, expressed his intention to conclude and bring into force by April 1952, agreements with state governments appointing the bank as their sole banker as well as, wherever practicable, consequent subsidiary agreements for appointing state banks as its agents.

The Rural Credit Survey recommended the amalgamation by statute of ten major state banks and four minor state banks with the proposed State Bank of India. The major state banks recommended for amalgamation were the State Bank of Saurashtra, the Bank of Patiala, the Bank of Bikaner, the Bank of Jaipur, the Bank of Rajasthan, the Bank of Indore, the Bank of Baroda, the Bank of Mysore, the Hyderabad State Bank, and the Travancore Bank. While identifying the Sangli Bank, the Manipur State Bank, the Bank of Baghelkhand, and the Mayurbhanj State Bank as the four minor state banks which could be brought into the fold of the State Bank of India, the Report of the Rural Credit Survey also advised the bank and the government to explore the possibility of merging some of the remaining minor state Banks with the State Bank of India.

The State Bank of India (Subsidiary Banks) Bill, 1959 was introduced in Parliament on 4th March 1959, and was referred to a Joint Select Committee at the end of April 1959. The bill, as amended by the Select Committee, was passed by the Lok Sabha on August 12, 1959 and by the Rajya Sabha the following week. With the President assenting to the legislation early in September 1959, the decks were cleared to take over the major state-associated banks, vest their ownership in the State Bank of India, and reconstitute them as its subsidiaries.

Having already come under the bank's ownership, the State Bank of Hyderabad presented the least complications. It was the first state-associated bank to be reconstituted as a subsidiary of the State Bank of India and commencing business in that capacity on October 1, 1959.

The state banks of Bikaner, Indore, and Jaipur came into existence on 1st January 1960, and the other subsidiary banks were established during the course of the next few months. The State Bank of India's holdings of the shares of the new institutions ranged from 100 percent in the State Banks of Hyderabad, Patiala, and Saurashtra, to just over 81 percent and 75.5 percent respectively in the State Banks of Indore and Travancore, and about 58.5 percent in the State Bank of Mysore.

The State Bank of India (Subsidiary Banks) Act, 1959 was an Act to provide for the formation of certain government or government associated banks as subsidiary of the State Bank of India and for the constitution, management and control of the subsidiary banks so formed, and for matters connected therewith, or incidental thereto.

**4.1 State Bank of Bikaner and Jaipur**

The genesis of State Bank of Bikaner and Jaipur dates back to the year 1943-44, when the Bank of Jaipur Ltd. and the Bank of Bikaner Ltd. came into existence. In 1960, both banks were incorporated as subsidiaries of State Bank of India and named as State Bank of Bikaner and State Bank of Jaipur.

On January 1, 1963, both banks were merged into one entity viz. State Bank of Bikaner and Jaipur.

The constitution, capital, management and other matters pertaining to the bank are governed by the provisions of SBI (Subsidiary Banks) Act, 1959. 75 percent of the shares of SBBJ are held by SBI and the remaining by institutions and general public.

The bank took over the business of the Govind Bank Pvt. Ltd, Mathura on April 25, 1966. SBBJ went public in the year 1997-98 with an issue of 12.21 lakh shares of ₹ 100 each at a premium of ₹ 440. SBBJ is the only public sector bank with headquarters in Rajasthan. At the time of incorporation, the bank had a business of ₹ 45 crore, net profit of ₹ 7.5 lakh and a network of 124 branches (96 in Rajasthan). By March 2012, the business of the bank increased to ₹ 1,11,558 crore, net profit stood at ₹ 652.03 crore and the number of branches increased to 950. SBBJ had sponsored three regional rural banks viz. Marwar Gramin Bank (set up in 1976), Sriganganagar Kshetriya Gramin Bank (1984) and Bikaner Kshetriya Gramin Bank (1985). These have since been merged into single RRB viz. MGB Gramin Bank in June 2006. The bank shoulders lead bank responsibility in 9 districts of the State.

The bank has engrained its ethos, values, culture and aspirations in its vision and mission statements. The vision and mission statements were last revised in the year 2000 and a need was felt to revise these statements keeping in view the changed market conditions. Accordingly, the statements were revised in the year 2009-10 and the revised statements are as follows,

**4.1.1 Vision:** "To be a state-of-the-art, customer-centric, values driven and professionally managed banking organisation; committed to the highest standards of good corporate governance practices; perpetual enhancement of the wealth of the shareholders and welfare of all stakeholders and the society".

**4.1.2 Mission:** "To provide one stop solutions to all the banking needs of customers through a highly motivated, professional and efficient human resources pool with quality of service, customer care and customers' business in focus by efficient use of information technology in a cost effective manner; meeting the expectations of all stakeholders through transparent, true and fair disclosures and responsive management principles in all the activities; to strive to fulfil corporate social responsibility with special emphasis on financial inclusion throughout the State of Rajasthan and aiming to provide the best banking services to one and all".

The major distinguishing features of the revised vision and

mission statements were laying emphasis on being state-of-the-art bank, adopting good corporate governance practices, welfare of all stakeholders and the society, providing one stop solutions to customers, efficient use of information technology in a cost effective manner, transparent/true/fair disclosures, responsive management principles, fulfilling corporate social responsibility and implementing financial inclusion in the state of Rajasthan.

## 4.2 State Bank of Hyderabad

State Bank of Hyderabad was constituted as Hyderabad State Bank on August 8, 1941 under Hyderabad State Bank Act, 1941. The bank started with the unique distinction of being the central bank of the erstwhile State of Hyderabad, covering present-day Telangana region of Andhra Pradesh, Hyderabad-Karnataka of Karnataka and Marathwada of Maharashtra, to manage its currency–Osmania Sikka and public debt apart from the functions of commercial banking. The first branch of the Bank was opened at Gun Foundry, Hyderabad on 5th April, 1942.

In 1953, the bank took over the assets and liabilities of the Hyderabad Mercantile Bank Ltd. In the same year, the bank started conducting government and treasury business as agent of Reserve Bank of India. In 1956, the bank was taken over by Reserve Bank of India as its first subsidiary and its name was changed from Hyderabad State Bank to State Bank of Hyderabad. The bank became a subsidiary of the State Bank of India on the 1st October 1959 and is now the largest associate bank of State Bank of India.

**4.2.1 Mission:** "To achieve pre-eminence in banking and financial sectors with commitment to excellence in customer satisfaction, profit maximisation and continued emphasis on developmental banking through a skilled and committed work force by providing training facilities and technological up-gradation".

**4.3 State Bank of Mysore**

In 1913, at the instance of Sir M. Visvesvaraya, the Engineer Statesman, a state-aided bank, under the patronage of His Highness the Maharaja of Mysore, Sri Krishnaraja Wodeyar IV, was established. This was "Mysore Bank Ltd.". During 1953, "Mysore Bank" was appointed as an agent of Reserve Bank of India to undertake government business and treasury operations, and in March 1960, it became a subsidiary of the State Bank of India under the State Bank of India (Subsidiary Banks) Act, 1959.

The bank has grown progressively, right from its inception and has declared uninterrupted profits from the beginning. "Mysore Bank", as it is popularly known, is constantly committed to serve its customers.

Bharata Ratna Sir M. Visvesvaraya

**4.4 State Bank of Patiala**

The rich heritage of State Bank of Patiala dates back to the year 1917, when it was founded by Late His Highness Bhupinder Singh, Maharaja of erstwhile Patiala State, with one branch by the name of 'Chowk Fort, Patiala' to begin with. The bank, then known as the 'Patiala State Bank' was state-owned and set up for the explicit purpose of fostering growth of agriculture, trade and industry. The constitution, scope and operations of the bank underwent a sea change with the formation of the Patiala and East Punjab States Union (PEPSU) in 1948. The bank was then reorganized and brought under the control of Reserve Bank of India.

It was christened as the Bank of Patiala. Another milestone

in history of the bank was its becoming a subsidiary of the State Bank of India on 1st April, 1960 when it was named as the State Bank of Patiala and since then it has grown significantly both in size and volume of business. During these glorious years, the bank has been playing an important role in banking sphere.

The bank has added a golden chapter to its history by fully networking all its branches on core banking solutions (CBS) on 08.08.2005 and became the first fully networked public sector bank in the country.

**4.5 State Bank of Travancore**

State Bank of Travancore (SBT) was originally established as Travancore Bank Ltd. in 1945 sponsored by the erstwhile princely state of Travancore. Under a special statute of the Indian Parliament (SBI Subsidiary Banks Act, 1959) it was made an associate of the State Bank of India and a member of the State Bank group.

SBI's five associate banks had a market share of 5.88 percent in deposits and 6.00 percent in advances as on last Friday of March 2011. State Bank of Indore, one of the associate banks, was acquired on 26th August 2010 after the final approval from RBI and GoI and State Bank of Saurastra was merged with State Bank of India on 13th September, 2008.

# 5

# Public Sector Banks

Nationalised banks dominate the banking system in India. The history of nationalised banks in India dates back to mid-20th century, when Imperial Bank of India was the first bank to be nationalised (under the SBI Act, 1955) and re-christened as State Bank of India (SBI) in July 1955. On July 19, 1960, eight banks of princely states were nationalized and became the seven subsidiaries of SBI with deposits of over ₹ 200 crore. These subsidiaries of SBI were State Bank of Bikaner and Jaipur (SBBJ), State Bank of Hyderabad (SBH), State Bank of Indore (SBIN), State Bank of Mysore (SBM), State Bank of Patiala (SBP), State Bank of Saurashtra (SBS), and State Bank of Travancore (SBT).

However, major nationalisation of banks happened in 1969 by the then Prime Minister Indira Gandhi. The objective behind nationalization of banks was to spread banking infrastructure to rural areas and make cheap finance available to Indian farmers. The 14 major commercial Banks with deposits of ₹ 50 crore were nationalized in 1969. In the year 1980, the second phase of nationalisation of Indian banks took place, in which 6 more banks with deposits of over ₹ 200 crore were nationalised. These banks were Allahabad Bank, Andhra Bank, Bank of Baroda, Bank of India, Bank of Maharashtra, Canara Bank, Central Bank of India, Corporation Bank, Dena Bank, Indian Bank, Indian Overseas Bank, New Bank of India, Oriental Bank of Commerce (OBC), Punjab and Sind Bank, Punjab National Bank (PNB), Syndicate Bank, UCO Bank, Union Bank of India, United Bank of India (UBI), and Vijaya Bank.

With this, the Government of India held control over 91 percent of the banking industry in India. After the nationalisation of banks, there was a huge jump in the deposits and advances with the banks. At present, the State Bank of India is the largest commercial Bank in India and is ranked as the 54th largest Bank worldwide. As at the end of March 2011, it served 140 million customers through a network of 13,542 branches and 25,005 Group ATMs.

**5.1 Allahabad Bank**

The oldest joint stock bank of the Country, Allahabad Bank was founded on April 24, 1865 by a group of Europeans at Allahabad. At that juncture, organized industry, trade and banking had started taking shape in India. Thus, the history of the bank is spread over three centuries—Nineteenth, Twentieth and Twenty-first.

On April 24, 1865, the bank was founded at the confluence city of Allahabad by a group of Europeans. In 1920, The P&O Banking Corporation took over the bank by acquiring its shares with a bid price of ₹ 436 per share and the head office of the bank shifted to Calcutta in 1923 on business considerations. On July 19, 1969, the Bank with 151 branches, deposits of ₹ 119 crore and advances of ₹ 82 crore was nationalized along with 13 other banks. In October, 1989, United Industrial Bank Ltd. was merged with Allahabad Bank and in 1991 All Bank Finance Ltd., a wholly-owned subsidiary for merchant banking was instituted.

In the 21st Century, the bank came out with an initial public offer (IPO) of 10 crore shares of face value ₹ 10 each, reducing Government shareholding to 71.16 percent in October 2002. There was a follow on public offer (FPO) of 10 crore equity shares of face value ₹ 10 each with a premium of ₹ 72, further reducing Government shareholding to 55.23 percent in April, 2005.

The bank transcended beyond the national boundary, opening a representative office at Shenzen, China in June, 2006. October 2006 saw the roll-out of the first branch under core banking solutions. The bank opened its first overseas branch at Hong Kong in February, 2007. The same year, the Bank's business crossed the ₹ 1,00,000 crore mark.

## 5.2 Andhra Bank

Andhra Bank was founded by the eminent freedom fighter and a multifaceted genius, Dr. Bhogaraju Pattabhi Sitaramayya. The bank was registered on 20th November 1923 and commenced business on November 28, 1923 with a paid-up capital of ₹ 1 lakh and an authorised capital of ₹ 10 lakh. Dr Bhogaraju Pattabhi Sitaramayya was born on November 24, 1880 in Gundugolanu village, West Godavari District in Andhra Pradesh. He was a renowned freedom fighter and a very illustrious personality.

The symbol of infinity denotes a bank that is prepared to do anything, to go to any lengths, for the customer.

The blue pointer on the top represents the philosophy of a bank that is always looking for growth and newer directions. The key hole represents safety and security and the chain indicates togetherness. The colours red and blue denote dynamism and solidity.

## 5.3 Bank of Baroda

It has a long and eventful journey of almost a century across 25 countries. Starting in 1908 from a small building in Baroda to its new hi-rise and hi-tech Baroda Corporate Centre in Mumbai, it is a saga of vision, enterprise, financial prudence and corporate governance.

It is a story scripted in corporate wisdom and social pride. It is a story crafted in private capital, princely patronage and state ownership. It is a story of ordinary bankers and their extraordinary contribution in the ascent of Bank of Baroda to the formidable heights of corporate glory. It is a story that needs to be shared with all those millions of people-customers, stakeholders, employees and the public at large-who in ample measure, have contributed to the making of an institution.

To be a top ranking national bank of international

standards committed to augmenting stake holders' value through concern, care and competence.

The banks new logo is a unique representation of a universal symbol. It comprises dual 'B' letterforms that hold the rays of the rising sun and is called the Baroda Sun.

The Sun is an excellent representation of what the bank stands for. It is the single most powerful source of light and energy–its far reaching rays dispel darkness to illuminate everything they touch. Bank of Baroda seeks to be the source that will help all its stakeholders realise their goals. For its customers, it seeks to be a one-stop, reliable partner who will help them address different financial needs. For its employees, it offers rewarding careers and for its investors and business partners, maximum return on their investment.

The single-colour, compelling vermillion palette has been carefully chosen, for its distinctiveness as it stands for hope and energy.

The bank is characterised by diversity. Its network of branches spans geographical and cultural boundaries and rural-urban divides. Its customers come from a wide spectrum of industries and backgrounds. The Baroda Sun is a fitting face for its brand because it is a universal symbol of dynamism and optimism–it is meaningful for many audiences and easily decoded by all.

The new corporate brand identity is much more than a cosmetic change. It is a signal that the bank recognizes and is prepared for new business paradigms in a globalised world. At the same time, it would always stay in touch with its heritage.

## 5.4 Bank of India

Bank of India was founded on 7th September, 1906 by a group of eminent businessmen from Mumbai. The bank was under private ownership and control till July 1969 when it was nationalised along with 13 other banks.

Beginning with one office in Mumbai, with a paid-up capital of ₹ 50 lakh and 50 employees, the bank has made rapid growth over the years and blossomed into a mighty institution with a strong national presence and sizable international operations. In business volume, the bank occupies a premier position among the nationalised banks.

The bank has 3752 branches in India spread over all states/ union territories including specialized branches. These branches are controlled through 50 zonal offices. There are 29 branches/offices (including five representative offices) and 3 subsidiaries and 1 joint venture abroad.

The bank came out with its maiden public issue in 1997 and follow on qualified institution placement in February 2008. Net worth of the bank in F.Y. 2010-11 has increased to ₹ 15,499.5 crore from ₹ 12,456 crore. During the year, the bank issued 2,13,04,870 equity shares of ₹ 10 each to Government of India at a price of ₹ 474.07 per share, on preferential basis, as approved by the shareholders in an extra ordinary general meeting held in accordance with Regulation 76(1) of SEBI (Issue of Capital and Disclosure Requirements) Regulations, 2009. The amount received by the Bank on this account was ₹ 1,010 crore. Consequently, the Government of India shareholding increased from 64.47 percent to 65.86 percent.

While firmly adhering to a policy of prudence and caution, the bank has been in the forefront of introducing various innovative services and systems. Business has been conducted with the successful blend of traditional values and ethics and the most modern infrastructure. The bank has been the first among the nationalised banks to establish a fully computerised branch and ATM facility at the Mahalaxmi branch at Mumbai way back in 1989. The bank is also a founder member of SWIFT in India. It pioneered the introduction of the Health Code System in 1982, for evaluating/rating its credit portfolio.

The bank's association with the capital market goes back to 1921 when it entered into an agreement with the Bombay Stock Exchange (BSE) to manage the BSE Clearing House. It is an association that has blossomed into a joint venture with

BSE, called the BOI Shareholding Ltd. to extend depository services to the stock broking community. Bank of India was the first Indian bank to open a branch outside the country at London in 1946, and also the first to open a branch in Europe at Paris in 1974. The bank has sizeable presence abroad, with a network of 29 branches (including five representative offices) at key banking and financial centres viz. London, New York, Paris, Tokyo, Hong Kong and Singapore. International business accounts for around 17.82 percent of the bank's total business.

**5.5 Bank of Maharashtra**

Maharashtra has a long history of commercial activity since ages because of its strategic location in the Indian sub-continent and its large natural resources.

Maharashtra has been a progressive region and banking activity was also started in this region quite early. Historically speaking, the Bank of Bombay established in 1840 was the first commercial bank in Maharashtra. However, the first commercial bank set up in Maharashtra outside Mumbai was The Poona Bank established in 1889 at Pune followed by The Deccan Bank in 1890 and the Bombay Banking Company in 1898. Mahratta Chamber of Commerce and Industries (MCCI) was founded by Late Mr. A.R. Bhat in 1934 to accelerate the industrial growth in and around Pune. Mr. Bhat was a journalist and an economist and was the general manager of the famous Marathi newspaper 'Kesari'.

Mr. Bhat initiated a comprehensive review of banking services available in the region through the special issue of Kesari newspaper released in memory of Lokmanya Tilak within a few months of establishment of MCC. He ensured that his friend, Shri V.P. Varde, considered as a doyen of cooperative movement, wrote an article on the necessity of a separate bank for Maharashtra, thus launching a public discussion on the subject. While there was no noticeable response to the article of Shri Varde, Shri A.R. Bhat kept on discussing the subject with leaders of trade and industry.

Mr. Bhat ensured that Mahratta Chamber and its directors took up the issue and held a conference on business and industry in Poona on behalf of the MCC in February, 1935.

Mr. Bhat pushed the proposal for formation of a bank and succeeded in getting the following resolution adopted by the Conference, "For providing capital to the trade and industry in Maharashtra, it is essential to establish a joint stock commercial bank. The Mahratta Chamber is, therefore, requested to make all the necessary enquiries in that behalf and take appropriate steps for floating such a bank. The business community in Maharashtra is urged to support such an effort". The Swadeshi movement in the first decade of the 20th Century gave stimulus to the establishment of a number of commercial banks under Indian management in Maharashtra. The MCC formed a sub-committee consisting of Sarvashri V.G. Kale, D.K. Sathe, N.G. Pawar, G.D. Apte and A.R. Bhat to work out the details.

The first meeting of the committee was held on 19 May 1935 in the conference room of the Kesari Mahratta office and besides the committee members, prominent personalities from the city like Shri Babasaheb Kamat, the then president of the MCCI, J. S. Karandikar, Rajabhau Godbole, Govindrao Pandit, Damuanna Potdar, S.R. Sardesai, Baburao Gokhale, and N.N. Kshirsagar among others participated in the deliberations.

Another meeting of the sub-committee with wider public representation was followed on May 27, 1935 in the meeting hall of Kesari Mahratta office and decisions on matters like the number of directors on the board of the proposed bank (maximum to be 11 members), amount of each share (to be ₹ 50) and primary condition for becoming a Director (to hold a minimum of 500 shares) were taken.

The bank was formally registered under the Indian Companies Act on the day of 16th September, 1935.

The bank commenced operations on 08-02-1936 in Pune and the second branch of the bank was opened in 1938 at Fort,

Bombay. The third branch came up at Deccan Gymkhana, Pune in the year 1940. In 1944, the status of a scheduled bank was obtained and in the year 1946 it formed a fully owned subsidiary, The Maharashtra Executor & Trustee Company and opened its first branch outside Maharashtra in Hubli (Mysore State, now Karnataka). In 1969, it was nationalised along with 13 other banks. In the year 1978, the new heod Office building was inaugurated by Hon'ble Prime Minister of India, Shri Morarji Desai. In 1979, "MahaBank Agricultural Research and Rural Development Foundation", registered as a public trust, was established for undertaking research and extension work and to provide more extensive services to farmers. In 1985, the 500th branch in Maharashtra state was opened at the hands of the then Prime Minister, Mrs. Indira Gandhi at Nariman Point, Mumbai.

**5.6 Canara Bank**

Widely known for customer centricity, Canara Bank was founded by Shri Ammembal Subba Rao Pai, a great visionary and philanthropist, in July 1906, at Mangalore, then a small port in Karnataka. Founded as 'Canara BankHindu Permanent Fund', this small seed blossomed into a limited company as 'Canara Bank Ltd.' in 1910 and became Canara Bank in 1969 after nationalization.

"A good bank is not only the financial heart of the community, but also one with an obligation of helping in every possible manner to improve the economic conditions of the common people"—*A. Subba Rao Pai.*

On July 1 1906, the Canara Hindu Permanent Fund Ltd. was formally registered with a capital of 2000 shares of ₹ 50 each, with 4 employees. In 1910, Canara Hindu Permanent Fund was renamed as Canara Bank Limited. On July 19, 1969, 14 major banks of the country, including Canara Bank, were nationalized. The 1000th branch was inaugurated in 1976 and the 1st overseas branch at London was inaugurated in 1983. In 1984, the Laksmi Commercial Bank Limited was merged with it and in 1985 Indo Hong Kong International Finance Limited was commissioned. Can Bank Mutual Fund and Canfin Homes were launched in 1987 and Can Bank Venture Capital Fund, was started in 1989.

Can Bank Factors Limited, the factoring subsidiary was launched in 1989-90. In 1995-96, Canara Bank became the first bank to be conferred with ISO 9002 certification for one of its branches in Bengaluru and in 2001-02, it opened a 'Mahila Banking Branch', first of its kind at Bengaluru, for catering exclusively to the financial requirements of women clientele. Maiden IPO of the bank came in 2002-03 and in 2006-07 it signed MoU for commissioning two JVs in insurance and asset management with international majors viz., HSBC (Asia Pacific) Holding and Robeco Group N.V respectively. In 2011-12, the bank's aggregate business crossed ₹ 5 lakh crore mark and 100 percent coverage under core banking solutions was achieved.

The bank's 4th foreign branch at Leicester and a representative office at Sharjah, UAE, were also opened. The bank raised ₹ 1993 crore under QIP and the government holding was reduced to 67.72 percent post QIP.

## 5.7 Central Bank of India

Established in 1911, Central Bank of India was the first Indian commercial bank which was wholly-owned and managed by Indians. The establishment of the bank was the ultimate realisation of the dream of Sir Sorabji Pochkhanawala, founder of the bank. Sir Pherozesha Mehta was the first Chairman of a truly 'Swadeshi Bank'. In fact, such was the extent of pride felt by Sir Sorabji Pochkhanawala that he proclaimed Central Bank of India as the 'property of the nation and the country's asset'. He also added that 'Central Bank of India lives on people's faith and regards itself as the people's own bank'.

Sorabji Pochkhanawala, though only twenty eight had been a banker for twelve years. He was the first Indian to be a certificated associate of the Institute of Bankers, London. Though he had discharged, when required, the duties of a manager of a bank, he was not recognised as one. Nor was he given employment as "manager" when he applied for that position at various banks such as the Bombay Merchants Bank because of the "deeply entrenched notion that 'native gentlemen' would be unable to conduct a bank according to western principles and that natives will not trust natives". On leaving Bank of India, Mr. Pochkhanawala with the support of a prominent cotton merchant, Mr. Kalianji Varadhman Jetsey rented premises formerly occupied by the Eastern Bank for ₹ 600 per month in the Gresham Building. He purchased two chairs and tables and began planning.

The bank's first employee was Mr. Sorabji Vicaji as Chief Cashier at ₹ 500 per month. The memorandum and articles of association were drawn up and the bank was registered on December 21, 1911. The birth of Central Bank of India is unique in Indian banking history. While other Indian banks were established by Englishmen or wealthy businessmen and managed by Europeans, this was the first bank established by Indians and managed by Indians.

At the meeting of the Directors held on December 28, 1911 the relevant article was amended and a formal invitation was sent to Sir Pherozeshah Mehta. Sir Mehta accepted the invitation and the first meeting he chaired was on January 12, 1912. The fact that a man of Sir Mehta's eminence had consented to become chairman helped the bank's acceptance among the public immeasurably. On March 15, 1912 the share list was closed and the bank's capital of ₹ 20 lakh was fully subscribed. An old directory of that time states, "this banking institution was commenced at Bombay in December 1911 with an authorized capital of ₹ 50,00,000 divided into 1,00,000 shares of ₹ 50 each while its subscribed capital amounted to ₹ 20,00,000 one half of which was paid up. The bank very quickly secured the confidence of the public owing to the sound financial position of its directors and the business-like manner in which its officials conducted its affairs". The bank began its operations in Gresham Building. On the opening day, a large number of merchants visited the bank. By the end of the first week, the bank had over seventy current accounts aggregating Rupees one and a half lakh. As business expanded, its main Mumbai branch moved to Alice Building in Horn by Road (presently Dr. Dadabhai Naoroji Road) on February 15, 1915 and then to the Taj Building on the same road in March 1921.

In 1923, after the merger of Tata Industrial Bank, the bank shifted to the magnificent premises designed by George Wittet occupied by that Bank on Esplanade Road (presently Mahatma Gandhi Marg).The bank's first branch outside of Mumbai was opened in Karachi in August 1913. In Kolkata, the bank began its operations in 1916. Until 1923, the bank had only 19 branches. This grew gradually to 23 by 1929 and 29 by 1932. However, there was a spurt and in 1933, 34 branches were opened. It grew to 88 branches by 1937 when there were more branches opened and by 1943, the bank had 217 branches.

In 1947, the Chairman of Central Bank of India, Sir Homi Mody was the main person responsible for the creation of the Indian Banks' Association-the key body of bankers in India. This was the realisation of a dream of Sir Pochkhanawala. In the thirties, Sir Pochkhanawala had wanted to bring directors and executives of Indian banks together on a common forum to exchange ideas, formulate policies and regulate bankers' behaviour and attitudes on the basis of some norms.

### 5.8 Corporation Bank

Every institution has its start in modest initiatives but what makes it great is the passion of the people behind it. Carrying the legacy forward with an undaunted commitment to its vision, the journey of Corporation Bank truly epitomizes this. Started in 1906, with an initial capital of just ₹ 5,000, Corporation Bank has recorded ₹ 2,00,000 crore mark in business, with over 5,000 service outlets across the nation, served by committed and dedicated 13,000 plus Corp Bankers, proof of which is seen in its enviable track record in financial performance. It has many reasons to cheer, predominant of them is, being able to participate in nation building by empowering the rural and urban population alike. Today, it is proud to be a significant contributor to the growth of the country's economy.

Corporation Bank came into being as Canara Banking Corporation (Udupi) Limited, on March 12, 1906, in the temple town of Udupi, by the pioneering efforts of a group of visionaries. The bank started functioning with just ₹ 5,000 as its capital and at the end of the first day, the resources stood at 38 Rupees-13 Annas-2 Pies.

The founder president Khan Bahadur Haji Abdullah Haji Kasim Saheb Bahadur was committed to fulfil the long felt banking needs of the people as well as inculcate the habit of savings and provided the much-needed impetus to founding a financial institution that would bring about prosperity to society.

The content of the first appeal to the public dated February 19, 1906 speaks volumes about the lofty ideals and ethos behind the foundation. The founder president Haji Abdullah declared that "the primary object in forming 'Corporation' is not only to cultivate habits of thrift amongst all classes of people, without distinction of caste or creed, but also habits of co-operation amongst all classes". "This is 'Swadeshism' pure and simple and every lover of the country is expected to come forward and co-operate in achieving this end in view".

The initial growth was consciously cautious and need based. The first branch of the bank was opened at Kundapur in 1923, followed by the second in Mangalore in 1926. The Bank stepped into the then Coorg State in 1934 by opening its seventh branch at Madikeri. In 1937, the bank was included in the second schedule of Reserve Bank of India Act, 1934. In 1939, the bank's name changed from Canara Banking Corporation (Udipi) Ltd., to "Canara Banking Corporation

Ltd.," and strongly put forth its vision with the motto "Sarve Janah Sukhino Bhavantu" which means "Prosperity to All".

The second change in the name of the bank occurred in 1972, from 'Canara Banking Corporation Ltd.' to 'Corporation Bank Limited' and finally 'Corporation Bank' following its nationalization on April 15, 1980. Corporation Bank was the forerunner when it came to evolving and adapting to the financial sector reforms. In 1997, it became the second public sector bank in the country to enter the capital market, the IPO of which was oversubscribed 13 times. The bank has many "firsts" to its credit—cash management services, gold banking, m-commerce, online approvals for educational loans, 100 percent CBS compliance and more recently, its pioneering efforts to take technology to the rural masses in remotest villages through low-cost branchless banking-Business Correspondent Model. All of this symbolizes the bank's commitment to its customers to provide convenience banking.

The Bank's motto "*Sarve Janah Sukhino Bhavanthu*" in Sanskrit, which means "Prosperity for All" is well-professed by the bank in its day-to-day operations. The bank's logo has various components, namely *Kamadhenu* (denoting wish-fulfilment), *Kalpatharu* (eternity), balance (justice for all), wheel (industrial progress) and wheat grains (agricultural prosperity) which stand for universal prosperity and as a wish-fulfilling credo. The logo in its present form was incorporated in 1972 when the name of the bank was changed from Canara Banking Corporation (Udipi) Ltd. to Corporation Bank Ltd.

### 5.9 Dena Bank

Dena Bank was founded on 26th May, 1938 by the family of Devkaran Nanjee under the name Devkaran Nanjee Banking Company Ltd. It became a public limited company in December 1939 and later the name was changed to Dena Bank Ltd. In July, 1969 Dena Bank Ltd. along with 13 other major banks was nationalized and is now a public sector bank constituted under the Banking Companies (Acquisition and

Transfer of Undertakings) Act, 1970. Under the provisions of the Banking Regulation Act, 1949, in addition to the business of banking, the bank can undertake other business as specified in Section 6 of the Banking Regulation Act, 1949.

The logo of Dena Bank depicts Goddess Lakshmi, the Goddess of Wealth, according to Hindu mythology. It was the desire of the founding fathers of the bank that the bank should be a symbol of prosperity for all its clients, and the logo represents this promise.

The contemporary 'D' in the logo reflects the dynamism, dedication and the drive towards customer satisfaction.

**5.10 Indian Bank**

Indian Bank (IB) was founded by Annamalai and Ramaswami Chettiar on August 15, 1907 as part of the Swadeshi movement. This was in response to the financial crash faced by two leading trading companies in Madras, Arbuthnot's and Binny's. Indian Bank began its international expansion in 1932 when it opened a branch in Colombo. A branch in Jaffna followed three years later, but this was not successful and was closed in 1939. Just before World War II reached the region, Indian Bank opened a branch in 1940 in Rangoon (Yangon).

The next year it closed the Rangoon branch, but opened branches in Singapore [where future branch manager K.B. Pisharody (1915–1998) started his career in the same year], and in Kuala Lumpur, Ipoh, and Penang. The rapid advance of the Japanese Army forced IB to close all its branches in Malaya and Singapore. Although the Japanese forces did not reach Ceylon, IB closed the Colombo branch in 1942. After the War, it reopened its Malayan and Singapore branches. In 1948, it reopened its branch in Colombo.

The 1960s saw expansion on the domestic front as it acquired Mannargudi Bank (est. 1932) and Salem Bank (est. 1925). On 19 July 1969, the Government of India nationalized 14 top banks, including Indian Bank. In 1973, Indian Bank,

Indian Overseas Bank, and United Commercial Bank established the United Asian Bank Berhad in response to a new banking law in Malaysia that prohibited foreign government banks from operating in the country. International expansion continued in 1978 with IB becoming a technical adviser to PT Bank Rama in Indonesia, the result of the merger of PT Bank Masyarakat and PT Bank Ramayana. Two years later, IB, Bank of Baroda, and Union Bank of India established IUB International Finance, a licensed deposit taker in Hong Kong. Each of the three banks took an equal share in the joint venture. In 1987, IB made acquisitions when it rescued Bank of Tanjore (Bank of Thanjavur) in Tamil Nadu.

Indian Bank has its overseas branches in Singapore, Colombo including a foreign currency banking unit at Colombo and Jaffna and has 240 overseas correspondent banks in 70 countries.

The subsidiaries of Indian Bank are as follows:

1. IndBank Merchant Banking Services Ltd.
2. IndBank Housing Ltd.
3. IndFund Management Ltd.

IB is a front runner in specialised banking with 97 forex authorised branches inclusive of 1 specialised overseas branch at Chennai exclusively for handling forex transactions arising out of export, import, remittances and non-resident Indian business, and 62 special SME branches extending finance exclusively to SSI units.

**5.11 Indian Overseas Bank**

Indian Overseas Bank (IOB) was founded on 10th February 1937, by Shri M. Chidambaram Chettyar, a pioneer in many fields—banking, insurance and industry with the twin objectives of specialising in foreign exchange business and overseas banking. IOB had the unique distinction of commencing business on February 10, 1937 (on the inaugural day itself) in three branches simultaneously-at Karaikudi and Chennai in India and Rangoon in Burma (presently Myanmar) followed by a branch in Penang. At the dawn of Independence, IOB had 38 branches in India and 7 branches abroad. Deposits stood at ₹ 6.64 crore and advances at ₹ 3.23 crore at that time.

During the period, IOB expanded its domestic activities and enlarged its international banking operations. As early as 1957, the bank established a training centre which has now grown into a staff college at Chennai and 9 training centres all over the country. IOB was the first bank to venture into consumer credit. It introduced the popular personal loan scheme.

In 1964, the bank made a beginning in computerisation in the areas of inter-branch reconciliation and provident fund accounts. In 1968, IOB established a full-fledged department to cater exclusively to the needs of the agriculture sector.

IOB was one of the 14 major banks that was nationalised in 1969. On the eve of Nationalisation in 1969, IOB had 195 branches in India with aggregate deposits of ₹ 67.70 crore and advances of ₹ 44.90 crore. In 1973, IOB had to wind up its five Malaysian branches as the banking law in Malaysia prohibited operation of foreign government owned banks. This led to creation of United Asian Bank Berhad in which IOB had 16.67 percent of the paid up capital. In the same year, Bharat Overseas Bank Ltd. was created in India with 30 percent equity participation from IOB to take over IOB's branch at Bangkok in Thailand. In 1977, IOB opened its branch in Seoul and the bank opened a foreign currency banking unit in the free trade zone in Colombo in 1979.

The bank has sponsored 3 regional rural banks viz. Puri Gramya Bank, Pandyan Grama Bank, and Dhenkanal Gramya Bank. IOB started its website during the month of February 1997. IOB had the distinction of being the first bank in the banking industry to obtain ISO 9001 Certification for its computer policy and planning Department from Det Norske Veritas (DNV), Netherlands in September 1999. This certification covered design, development, implementation and maintenance of software developed in-house, procurement and supply of hardware and execution of turnkey projects.

The bank made a successful debut in raising capital from the public during the financial year 2000-01, despite a subdued capital market. The issue opened on September 25, 2000 for raising ₹ 111.20 crore and was oversubscribed by 1.87 times. Consequent to the public issue, the share of the Government in the bank's capital came down to 75 percent.

The shares of the Bank have been listed on the Madras Stock Exchange (Regional), Bombay Stock Exchange and the National Stock Exchange of India Ltd.

IDRBT (Institute for Development and Research in Banking Technology) conferred the best award under banking technology to IOB. The award was given for the innovative use of banking applications on INFINET (Indian Financial Network) for the year 2001.

Mobile banking under SMS technology has been implemented in Ahmedabad and Baroda. IOB was one among the first to join Reserve Bank of India's negotiated dealing system for security dialling online.

The bank has finalised an e-commerce strategy and has developed the necessary internet banking modules in-house. For the first time, total branch automation package developed in-house has been customised in one of the overseas branches of the bank.

### 5.12 Oriental Bank of Commerce

Oriental Bank of Commerce was primarily based in Lahore (then a city of British India, and now in Pakistan). It is amongst the leading public sector banks in India. Oriental Bank of Commerce made a beginning under its founding father, Late Rai Bahadur Lala Sohan Lal, the primary chairman of the bank. OBC was established in 1943 as the Oriental Bank of Commerce Limited at Lahore. In 1945, the bank was acquired by the "Thapar Group", a business group in the country at that time.

Within four years of stepping into existence, the bank

faced partition. Branches within the newly formed Pakistan had to be closed down and the registered workplace needed to be shifted from Lahore. The registered office of the bank was shifted to Delhi in 1950.

Late Lala Karam Chand Thapar, the then chairman of the Oriental Bank of Commerce, in a singular gesture honoured the commitments made to the depositors from Pakistan and paid every rupee to its departing customers. The bank has witnessed many ups and downs after its establishment.

The period of 1970-76 is stated to be the most difficult part in the historical past of the bank. At one time revenue plummeted that made the proprietor of the bank, the Thapar House, to consider closing the bank.

The employees and leaders of the bank came together to rescue the bank. Their efforts bore result and efficiency of the bank progressed significantly. This was the turning point in the history of the bank.

The bank was nationalized on April 15, 1980 and became a public sector bank. The Oriental Bank of Commerce was constituted through an Act of Parliament on July 11, 1980. The number of branches grew from 517 at the time of nationalisation in 1980 to 1,121 by December 31, 2004.

In 1994, it was the first nationalised bank to tap the capital market with a public issue of 60 million equity shares of ₹ 10 each at a premium of ₹ 50 per share aggregating ₹ 3600 million.

Punjab Cooperative Bank Limited and Bari Doaba Bank Limited were amalgamated with OBC with effect from 8th April 1997. 10 branches of these two banks which were taken over re-started their operations as Oriental Bank of Commerce branches w.e.f. May 8, 1997.

Global Trust Bank, a private sector bank, was amalgamated with OBC as per the scheme formulated by the GoI, effective from August 14, 2004.

The correspondent network of the bank consisting of 138 major banks all over the world and 27 NOSTRO Accounts enables the bank to meet the foreign exchange requirements of its clientele. Oriental Bank of Commerce (OBC) is the first public sector bank in the country to join hands with Citibank to launch OBC co-branded credit card. The formal agreement to this effect was signed between the two partners on July 27, 1998.

The bank joined hands with Infosys Technologies Ltd. and Wipro Ltd. for its centralised banking solution (CBS). Small Industries Development Bank of India (SIDBI) entered into alliance with the Oriental Bank of Commerce (OBC) to jointly work on projects in the field of small-scale, infrastructure and service areas.

### 5.13 Punjab and Sind Bank

In 1908, leading figures such as Bhai Vir Singh, Sir Sunder Singh Majitha and Sardar Tarlochan Singh founded Punjab and Sind Bank to help the weaker sections of the society. The bank was incorporated as 'The Punjab and Sind Bank Limited' on June 24, 1908, with its registered office situated at Hall Bazar, Amritsar, Punjab, India. Punjab and Sind Bank was one of the few banks in northern India that honoured its obligations to Hindu clients that left Pakistan and migrated to India at the time of partition even though the bulk of its operations had been in Pakistan and it had only a few branches in India.

On April 15, 1980 Punjab and Sind Bank was one of the six banks that the Government of India nationalized in the second wave of nationalization (The first wave had been in 1969 when the Government nationalized the top 14 Banks). The bank was constituted as a 'corresponding new bank' on April 15, 1980, as defined under Section 2(b) of the Bank Acquisition Act. The central and administrative office of the bank at the time of constitution under the Bank Acquisition Act was situated at New Delhi.

At some point in the 1960s, Punjab and Sind Bank established a branch in London. In 1991, Bank of Baroda acquired Punjab and Sind Bank's London branch at the behest of the Reserve Bank of India following Punjab and Sind Bank's involvement in the Sethia fraud in 1987.

Since 2004, Punjab and Sind Bank has again shown growth of more than 40 percent year on year. Recently, its IPO received tremendous response from the public and the issue was oversubscribed by more than 50 times. Recently, the bank crossed the mark of ₹ 1,00,000 crore in business.

The bank has entered into agreements for non-life insurance business with Bajaj Allianz General Insurance Company and life insurance business arrangements with Aviva Life Insurance Company India Pvt. Ltd. Punjab and Sind Bank (PSB) has inked a pact with Wipro, for a 10 year contract for comprehensive IT outsourcing services for PSB in 2010.

**5.14 Punjab National Bank**

At the instance of Rai Mool Raj, Lala Lajpat Rai sent a circular to selected friends insisting on an Indian joint stock bank as the first special step in constructive Swadeshi. Lala Harkrishan Lal who had returned from England with ideas regarding commerce and industry, was eager to give them practical shape.

On May 23, 1894, the efforts materialized. The founding board was drawn from different parts of India professing different faiths and a varied background with, however, the common objective of providing the country with a truly national bank which would further the economic interest of the country.

The bank opened for business on April 12, 1895. The first board of 7 directors comprised of Sardar Dayal Singh Majithia, who was also the founder of Dayal Singh College and the Tribune; Lala Lalchand one of the founders of DAV College and President of its Management Society; Kali Prosanna Roy, eminent Bengali pleader who was also the Chairman of the reception committee of the Indian National Congress at its Lahore session in 1900; Lala Harkishan Lal who became widely known as the first industrialist of Punjab; EC Jessawala, a well-known Parsi merchant and partner of Jamshedji and Co. of Lahore; Lala Prabhu Dayal, a leading Rais, merchant and philanthropist of Multan; Bakshi Jaishi Ram, an eminent civil lawyer of Lahore; and Lala Dholan Dass, a great banker, merchant and Rais of Amritsar. Thus, a Bengali, Parsi, a Sikh and a few Hindus joined hands in a purely national and cosmopolitan spirit to establish this bank which opened its doors to the public on 12th April, 1895. They went about it with a missionary zeal. Shri Dayal Singh Majithia was the first chairman, Lala Harkishan Lal, the first secretary to the Board and Shri Bulaki Ram Shastri Barrister at Lahore, was appointed manager.

Incorporated under the Act VI of 1882 Indian Companies Act, the bank commenced operations on April 12, 1895 from Lahore, with an authorised total capital of ₹ 2 lakh and working capital of ₹ 20,000.

The first branch outside Lahore was opened in Rawalpindi in 1900. The bank made slow, but steady progress in the first decade of its existence. Lala Lajpat Rai joined the board of directors soon after. In 1913, the banking industry in India was hit by a severe crisis following the failure of the Peoples Bank of India founded by Lala Harkishan Lal. As many as 78 banks failed during this crisis. Punjab National Bank survived. The years 1926 to 1936 were turbulent and loss ridden ones for the banking industry the world over. The 1929 Wall Street crash plunged the world into a severe economic crisis.

It was during this period that the Jalianwala Bagh Committee account was opened in the bank, which in the decade that followed, was operated by Mahatma Gandhi and Pandit Jawaharlal Nehru. The five years from 1941 to 1946 were ones of unprecedented growth. From a modest base of 71, the number of branches increased to 278. Deposits grew from ₹ 10 crore to ₹ 62 crore. On March 31, 1947, the bank officials decided to leave Lahore and transfer the registered office of the bank to Delhi and permission for transfer was obtained from the Lahore High Court on June 20, 1947.

PNB was then housed in the precincts of Sreeniwas in the salubrious Civil Lines, Delhi. Many a staff member fell victim to the widespread riots in the discharge of their duties. The conditions deteriorated further.

The bank was forced to close 92 offices in West Pakistan constituting 33 percent of the total number and having 40 percent of the total deposits. The bank, however, continued to maintain a few caretaker branches. The registered office was shifted to Delhi and the bank honoured all the deposit claims of the refugees even on the basis of whatever little evidence they could produce. Subsequently, the bank registered impressive performance and grew from strength to strength. The bank then embarked on the task of rehabilitating the displaced account holders.

The migrants from Pakistan were repaid their deposits based upon whatever evidence they could produce. Such gestures cemented their trust in the bank and PNB became a symbol of trust and a name they could bank upon. Surplus staff posed a big problem. Fast expansion became a priority. The policy paid rich dividends by opening up an era of phenomenal growth.

In 1951, the bank took over the assets and liabilities of Bharat Bank Ltd. and became the second largest bank in the private sector. In 1962, it amalgamated the Indo-Commercial Bank with it. From its dwindled deposits of ₹ 43 crore in 1949, it rose to cross the ₹ 355 crore mark by July 1969. Nationalisation came in 1969 which unleashed a new chapter in the long history of the bank. Keeping with the economic ideology of catalyzing development and alleviation of poverty by funding various self-employment schemes, PNB expanded its presence rapidly in un-banked areas. With its large presence throughout the country and with a view to strengthening the rural credit delivery system, the bank sponsored regional rural banks (RRBs).

The bank's growth has been aided by takeover/merger of 7

private sector banks during different periods in its history. The first ever and the only merger of a nationalized bank with PNB was in 1993 viz., New Bank of India. By late 1980s when the first whiff of liberalization came about, the bank initiated strategic moves towards diversification. In 2002, 20 percent of government ownership was disinvested through a very successful IPO to the public. In 2003, the erstwhile Nedungadi Bank Ltd (e-NBL), a Kerala based private bank was amalgamated with Punjab National Bank. This was the seventh merger in PNB's history of more than 115 years. PNB's management team has been quite successful in managing the mergers and ensuring the integration process in a smooth and effective manner. It may be added that no other bank in the nationalized bank group has a track record of so many mergers.

This has improved the franchise value of the bank, particularly, in the relatively under-represented Kerala region. In order to meet future capital requirements on account of implementation of Basel II norms, in March 2005, the bank came out with a follow-on public offer (FPO) through the book building process, reducing the shareholding of Government of India to 57.8 percent. Its number of offices increased to 569 and advances from ₹ 19 crore in 1949 to ₹ 243 crore by July 1969 when it was nationalised.

Since inception in 1895, PNB has always been a "People's Bank" serving millions of people throughout the country and also had the proud distinction of serving great national leaders like Sarvshri Jawahar Lal Nehru, Gobind Ballabh Pant, Lal Bahadur Shastri, Rafi Ahmed Kidwai, Smt. Indira Gandhi etc. amongst others who banked with them.

During 2008-09, the bank achieved the landmark of becoming the largest nationalized bank to bring all branches/extension counters into core banking solution (CBS).

### 5.15 Syndicate Bank

Syndicate Bank was established in 1925 in Udupi, the

abode of Lord Krishna in coastal Karnataka with a capital of ₹ 8000 by three visionaries—Shri Upendra Ananth Pai, a businessman, Shri Vaman Kudva, an engineer and Dr. T.M.A. Pai, a physician—who shared a strong commitment to social welfare. Their objective was primarily to extend financial assistance to the local weavers who were crippled by a crisis in the handloom industry through mobilising small savings from the community. The bank collected as low as 2 annas daily at the doorsteps of the depositors through its agents under its pigmy deposit scheme started in 1928. This scheme is the bank's brand equity today and the bank collects around `2 crore per day under the scheme.

On November 10, 1925, the business of the bank commenced in Udupi with the name "Canara Industrial and Banking Syndicate Ltd.," a joint stock company with just one employee. First branch of the bank opened at Brahmavar in Dakshina Kannada District in 1928. In 1937, the bank became a member of the clearing house for the first time at Bombay. In 1946, 29 branches opened in a single day in rural areas. It took over the assets and liabilities of 2 local banks viz. Maharashtra Apex Bank Ltd. and Southern India Apex Bank Ltd. 20 Banks merged with the bank during the period 1953-1964. In 1957, 100th branch was opened at Ilkal in Karnataka and in 1962 it entered foreign exchange business by opening foreign exchange department at Bombay. In 1963, the name of the Bank was changed from "Canara Industrial and Banking Syndicate Ltd." to "Syndicate Bank Limited". The head office was shifted to Manipal on April 19, 1964.

The bank was nationalised on July 19, 1969. It was acknowledged as a live example of mass banking and as a powerful catalyst of social change. Nationalisation, therefore, merely meant change of ownership. Bank had 306 branches at the time of nationalisation of which 66 percent were in rural and semi-urban centres. It opened a branch at Port Blair in Andaman and Nicobar islands. In 1970, the first staff training college was started at head office and in 1972 it opened a branch at Lakshadweep islands. The first overseas branch was opened at London on 17th August 1976.

## 5.16 UCO BANK

The idea of a truly Indian bank was conceived by Mr. G.D. Birla, the doyen of Indian industrial renaissance, after the historic "Quit India" movement in 1942. Soon this nascent idea came into reality and, on the 6th January 1943, the United Commercial Bank Ltd. was born with its registered and head office at Kolkata. The very first board of directors was represented by eminent personalities of the country drawn from all walks of life, and this all-India character of the bank has been assiduously maintained till this day. The bank was nationalized by the Government of India on the July 19, 1969 whereupon 100 percent ownership was taken over by the government in United Commercial Bank.

This historic event brought about a sea-change in the entire fabric of the bank's thinking and activities, commensurate with the government's socio-political approach of mass banking as against class banking hitherto practiced. Branch expansion started at a fast pace, particularly in rural areas, and the bank achieved several unique distinctions in priority sector lending and other social upliftment activities. To keep pace with the developing scenario and expansion of business, the bank undertook an exercise in organizational restructuring in the year 1972. The year 1985 opened a new chapter for the bank as the name of the bank was changed to UCO Bank by an Act of the Parliament. The customer friendly and socially committed character, however, remained even with this change in name which has, over the years, been regarded as one of the well-known and vibrant banks in the country.

Headquartered in Kolkata, the bank has 35 regional offices spread all over India. Branches located in a geographical area report to the regional office having jurisdiction over that area. Today, with all its inner strengths, UCO Bank has come a long way to symbolize friendliness for customers and efficiency in its banking business.

### 5.17 Union Bank of India

Union Bank of India (UBI) was established on November 11, 1919 with its headquarters in the city of Bombay now known as Mumbai. The head office building of the bank in Mumbai was inaugurated by Mahatma Gandhi, the Father of the nation in the year 1921, and he said on the occasion:

"We should have the ability to carry on a big bank, to manage efficiently crore of rupees in the course of our national activities. Though we have not many banks amongst us, it does not follow that we are not capable of efficiently managing crore and tens of crore of rupees".

At the time of India's Independence in 1947, UBI still only had four branches, three in Mumbai and one in Saurashtra, all concentrated in key trade centres. After Independence, UBI accelerated its growth and by the time the government nationalized it in 1969, it had grown to 240 branches in 28 states.

In 1969, the bank was brought into existence by the Ordinance issued on 10th July, by the Central Government. In terms of the Ordinance, the undertaking of The Union Bank of India, Ltd., was nationalized under the Banking Companies (Acquisition and Transfer of Undertakings) Act, 1969. An Ordinance was promulgated which was later replaced by the Banking Companies (Acquisition and Transfer of Undertakings) Act, 1970 made effective retrospectively from July 19, 1969.

On the technology front, the bank has taken early initiatives and 100 percent of its branches are computerised. The bank has also introduced core banking solution with connectivity between branches. 100 percent of the business of the bank is under core banking solution making it a leader among its peers in infusion of technology.

Union Bank of India completed 91 glorious years on November 11, 2010. To celebrate this happy occasion, the

Bank has launched "Bankers' Beacon-The Story of Union Bank of India".

This was released at a special function in Delhi on November 11, 2010 by Shri Pranab Mukherjee, Honourable Finance Minister, Government of India.

## 5.18 United Bank of India

On October 12, 1950, the name of Bengal Central Bank Limited (established in 1918 as Bengal Central Loan Company Limited) was changed to United Bank of India Limited for the purpose of amalgamation and on December 18, 1950, Comilla Banking Corporation Limited (established in 1914), the Camilla Union Bank Limited (established in 1922), the Hooghly Bank (established 1932) stood amalgamated with the bank. Subsequently, other banks namely, Cuttack Bank Limited, Tezpur Industrial Bank Limited, Hindustan Mercantile Limited and Narang Bank of India Limited were merged with the bank.

The origin of the bank thus goes as far back as to 1914. United Bank of India was constituted under the Banking Companies (Acquisition and Transfer of Undertakings) Act, 1970 on 19th July 1969.

The head office of the bank was set up at 4 Clive Ghat Street (presently known as N.C. Dutta Sarani, Kolkata) which was shifted to its present location at 11 Hemanta Basu Sarani, Kolkata in 1972 for operational efficiency. United Bank of India is one of the 14 banks which were nationalised on July 19, 1969. UBI played a significant role in the spread of banking services in different parts of the country, more particularly in Eastern and North-Eastern India. UBI has sponsored 4 regional rural banks (RRBs) one each in West Bengal, Assam, Manipur and Tripura. These four RRBs together have over 1000 branches. United Bank of India has contributed 35 percent of the share capital/additional capital to all the four RRBs in four different states.

**5.19 Vijaya Bank**

Vijaya Bank, was founded on October 23, 1931 by late Shri A.B. Shetty and other enterprising farmers in Mangalore, Karnataka. The objective of the founders was essentially to promote banking habit, thrift and entrepreneurship among the farming community of Dakshina Kannada district in Karnataka State. The bank became a scheduled bank in 1958.

Vijaya Bank steadily grew into a large all-India bank, with nine smaller banks merging with it during 1963-68. The credit for this merger as well as growth goes to late Shri M. Sunder Ram Shetty, who was then the chief executive of the bank. The bank was nationalised on April 15, 1980 and it has its headquarters in Bengaluru.

The bank has built a network of 1300 branches, 48 extension counters and 750 ATMs as on 31st March 2012, that span all 28 states and 4 union territories in the country. Vijaya Bank boasts of being one of the few banks which has undertaken the principal membership of VISA International and MasterCard International. Vijaya Bank has been constantly focusing on technological upgradation.

**5.20 Industrial Development Bank of India**

IDBI Bank Ltd. is today one of India's largest commercial banks. For over 40 years, IDBI Bank has essayed a key role in nation building, first as the apex development financial institution (DFI) (July 1, 1964 to September 30, 2004) and thereafter as a full-service commercial bank (October 1, 2004 onwards). As a DFI, the erstwhile IDBI stretched its canvas beyond mere project financing to cover an array of services that contributed towards balanced geographical spread of industries, development of identified backward areas and evolution of a deep and vibrant capital market. On October 1, 2004, the erstwhile IDBI converted into a banking company (as Industrial Development Bank of India Limited) to undertake the entire gamut of banking activities while continuing to play its secular DFI role.

Post the merger of the erstwhile IDBI Bank with its parent company (IDBI Ltd.) on April 2, 2005 and the subsequent merger of the erstwhile United Western Bank Ltd. with IDBI Bank on October 3, 2006, the tech-savvy, new generation bank with majority Government shareholding today touches the lives of millions of Indians through an array of corporate, retail, SME and agri-products and services. Headquartered in Mumbai, IDBI Bank today rides on the back of a robust business strategy, a highly competent and dedicated workforce and a state-of-the-art information technology platform, to structure and deliver personalised and innovative banking services and customised financial solutions to its clients across various delivery channels.

As on March 31, 2011, IDBI Bank has a balance sheet of ₹ 2.53 lakh crore and business size (deposits plus advances) of ₹ 3.38 lakh crore. As a universal bank, IDBI Bank, besides its core banking and project finance domain, has an established presence in associated financial sector businesses like capital market, investment banking and more recently, the mutual fund business.

In response to the felt need and on commercial prudence, it was decided to transform IDBI into a bank. For the purpose, Industrial Development Bank (transfer of undertaking and Repeal) Act, 2003 [Repeal Act] was passed repealing the Industrial Development Bank of India Act, 1964. In terms of the provisions of the Repeal Act, a new company under the name of Industrial Development Bank of India Limited (IDBI Ltd.) was incorporated as a government company under the Companies Act, 1956 on September 27, 2004. Thereafter, the undertaking of IDBI was transferred to and vested in IDBI Ltd. with effect from October 1, 2004. In terms of the provisions of the Repeal Act, IDBI Ltd. has been functioning as a bank in addition to its earlier role of a financial institution.

Towards achieving the faster inorganic growth of the bank, IDBI Bank Ltd., a wholly-owned subsidiary of IDBI Ltd. was amalgamated with IDBI Ltd. in terms of the provisions of

Section 44A of the Banking Regulation Act, 1949 providing for voluntary amalgamation of two banking companies. The merger became effective from 2nd April 2005.

The United Western Bank Ltd. (UWB), a Satara based private sector Bank was placed under moratorium by RBI. Upon IDBI Ltd. showing interest to take over the said bank towards its further inorganic growth, RBI and Government of India amalgamated UWB with IDBI Ltd. in terms of the provisions of Section 45 of the Banking Regulation Act, 1949. The merger came into effect on October 3, 2006.

In order that the name of the bank truly reflects the functions it is carrying on, the name of the bank was changed to IDBI Bank Limited and the new name became effective from May 7, 2008 upon issue of the fresh certificate of incorporation by Registrar of Companies, Maharashtra. The bank has been accordingly functioning in its present name of IDBI Bank Limited.

# 6

# Old Generation Private Sector Banks

Commercial banking in India can boast of a history of about 200 years. Though one could trace the history of banking back to the 19th century, the beginning of the last century saw the birth of many banks in India, set up by people with vision, commitment and national spirit. A brief introduction to the old generation private sector banks is given below.

## 6.1 Catholic Syrian Bank

With the Swadeshi Movement of early 20th century as its base, Catholic Syrian Bank was incorporated on 26th November 1920, in Thrissur district of Kerala. The Bank commenced its operations on 1st January 1921, with an authorized capital of ₹ 5 lakh and a paid up capital of ₹ 45,270. For the first two decades after its foundation, the Bank concentrated solely on Kerala. Following the crash of Travancore National Quilon Bank in 1938 and Palai Central Bank in 1960, many of the small-scale banks were on the verge of collapsing, laying down the path of consolidation, through mergers and acquisitions. It was in the decade of 1960 only, more specifically in 1964-65, that Catholic Syrian Bank Ltd. took over the liabilities and assets of five small/medium sized banks in Kerala, taking the very first step towards expansion. In August 1969, the bank attained the distinction of being included in the Second Schedule to the Reserve Bank of India Act, 1934. Six years later, in the year 1975, with its total deposits crossing the mark of ₹ 25 crore, the bank attained the status of Class 'A' scheduled bank.

Catholic Syrian Bank Ltd. started providing in house training to its staff by setting up of a training college in 1975. The very same year, the bank entered the field of foreign exchange. Data processing system was introduced in the bank and by November 1975, it started using IBM data processing machines for reconciliation of inter-branch accounts. The decade of 1970 also saw Catholic Syrian Bank open new branches, with emphasis on remote rural belts.

The bank also floated special schemes for catering to the credit needs of small-scale industries, road transport operators, agriculturists and other self-employed entrepreneurs. Even today, around 75 percent of the bank's clientele belongs to small and economically weaker sections of the society. Around 80 percent of its branches are in rural and semi-urban areas. At present, the bank is making investments in money market and capital market instruments and also trying to increase its market share of corporate finance. The Catholic Syrian Bank has a network of 364 branches and staff strength of 2,820.

### 6.2 Dhanlaxmi Bank

The foundation of Dhanlaxmi Bank Limited was laid on November 14, 1927, in the Thrissur district of Kerala. A group of innovative entrepreneurs had started the bank with a capital of 11,000 and only 7 employees. Fifty years later, in the year 1977, it became a scheduled commercial bank. The bank's corporate office, situated at Thrissur, and industrial finance branch, located in Kochi, has been accredited with certification under ISO 9001-2000. A professionally managed bank, Dhanlaxmi Bank boasts of substantial sophistication in its banking services. Dhanlaxmi Bank has a network of 275 branches which are spread over the states of Kerala, Tamil Nadu, Karnataka, Andhra Pradesh, Maharashtra, Gujarat, Delhi and West Bengal. At the same time, it has installed 401 networked ATMs in all those centres where high banking activity takes place. The main aim behind this is to provide easy banking access to the clients.

Dhanlaxmi Bank is one of those financial institutions that have moved ahead with the changing times. The centralised banking solution (CBS) on the Flexcube Platform, offered by the bank in all branches, allows its clients to reap the benefits of anywhere/anytime banking, through multiple delivery channels. The data centre of Dhanlaxmi Bank, set up in Bengaluru, keeps the networked system operational 24x7. Dhanlaxmi Bank, after its tie-up with Visa International, has introduced an international debit card for its clients. As a part of the effort, it has also joined CASHNET—the first independent nation-wide shared ATM network in India, National Financial Switch (ATM network) of the IDRBT-promoted by Reserve Bank of India and Cash Tree.

This allowed its clients, access to more than 25,000 ATMs in India. The bank has also ventured into life insurance (through MetLife India) and non-life insurance (through Oriental Insurance Co.). Being a depository participant of NSDL (National Security Depository Limited), Dhanlaxmi Bank offers demat services as well, though through selected branches only.

The tie-ups with UAE Exchange and Financial Services for Xpress Money and Moneygram, Wall Street Finance for Wall Street instant cash and IndusInd Bank Limited for Zoha Inc. ensure fast money transfer.

## 6.3 Federal Bank

Federal Bank Limited was founded as Travancore Federal Bank Limited in the year 1931, with an authorized capital of ₹ 5,000. It was established at Nedumpuram, a place near Tiruvalla, in Central Travancore (a princely state later merged into Kerala), under Travancore Company's Act. Thirteen years later, in 1944, Shri K. P. Hormis and his close relatives/friends took over the controlling interest in the bank. The following year, the paid-up capital of the Bank went up to ₹ 71,000 and its registered office shifted to Aluva, in Ernakulam district of Kerala. With the opening of its first branch at Aluva, Travancore Federal Bank commenced its business. It was in the board meeting of March 1947 that the name of the bank was changed to Federal Bank Limited. After a gap of 12 years i.e. in 1959, the bank was licensed under Section 22 of the Banking Companies Act, 1949. In 1964, it took over the liabilities of Chalakudy Public Bank Ltd. (Chalakudy), Cochin Union Bank Ltd. (Trichur) and Alleppey Bank Ltd. (Alleppey). In the next five years, Federal Bank took over St. George Union Bank Ltd. Puthenpally (1965) and Marthandom Commercial Bank Ltd. Trivandrum (1968). In 1970, it became a scheduled bank. Two years later, it became an authorized dealer in foreign exchange. Federal Bank came in an expansion mode and opened 53 branches in 1975 and 42 branches in 1976.

The year 1985 saw Federal Bank opening a personnel and industrial relations department and a computer department. Four years later, the bank entered the arena of merchant banking operations. In 1994, the bank came out with its first public issue, which was oversubscribed around 60 times. In the year 1997, Federal Bank inaugurated its first ATM, at Eranakulam North.

It was in the year 2000 that Federal Bank started the Any Where Banking (AWB) service in Bengaluru, followed by the depository Services, in association with NSDL. The same year, internet banking 'Fed Net' was launched, with the Federal Millennium CD being just in tow. With the start of 2001, the bank saw the launch of wide area network, connecting regional offices at Mumbai, Bengaluru, Chennai and Ernakulam as head office. The following year, all the branches of the bank were fully computerized (using Fed Soft).

In 2002, Federal Bank started the installation of switch for networking all the ATMs. Soon enough, it introduced Fed Alerts and Fed Mobile, with real-time transaction alerts and customizable options. Two years later, a call centre was set up by the bank, attached to the systems and technology department, and co-branded credit cards were launched, in association with ICICI Bank. In 2006, Federal Bank issued GDRs, becoming the first traditional Bank to do so.

### 6.4 Karnataka Bank

Karnataka Bank Limited, a scheduled commercial bank in India, was incorporated on 18th February 1924 at Mangalore, a coastal town of Dakshina Kannada district in Karnataka State. The bank took shape in the aftermath of patriotic zeal that engulfed the nation during the freedom movement of 20th Century.

During its process of expansion, the Karnataka Bank merged with other banks like Sringeri Sharada Bank Ltd., Chitradurga Bank Ltd. and Bank of Karnataka. Karnataka Bank has emerged as one of the top financial service institutions in India, with over 87 years of experience. It now has a national presence with a network of 489 branches spread across 20 states and 2 union territories. The bank has over 5,844 employees, 86,868 shareholders and over 4.84 million customers.

### 6.5 Karur Vysya Bank

The Karur Vysya Bank Limited, popularly known as KVB, was set up in 1916 by two great visionaries and illustrious sons of Karur, the Late Shri M.A. Venkatarama Chettiar and the Late Shri Athi Krishna Chettiar to inculcate the habit of savings and provide financial assistance to traders and small agriculturists in and around Karur, a textile town in Tamil Nadu.

Though the bank started with a seed capital of ₹ 1 lakh, it has withstood innumerable changes and challenges in the past few decades and has profitably emerged as one of the leading banks in India without compromising on its fundamentals. Shedding its inherent regional flavour, the bank has now spread its wings far and wide with over 320 branches in 13 states and 3 union territories in order to gain a pan India presence. The bank has been conducting its affairs meticulously to conform to all the prudential norms and exacting statutory regulations. The bank is professionally managed and guided by the board of directors drawn from different fields with vision, experience, knowledge and business acumen. KVB has also been generating profits and rewarding its stakeholders with handsome dividends since inception.

**6.6 South Indian Bank**

South Indian Bank Ltd. was established by a band of enterprising men at a time when Swadeshi movement was gathering momentum. The bank was established in Thrissur a major town in the erstwhile State of Cochin. The objective behind establishment of the bank was to provide for the people a safe, efficient and service oriented repository of savings of the community on one hand and to free the business community from the clutches of greedy moneylenders on the other by providing need based credit at reasonable rates of interest. ICICI Bank Ltd., is the biggest shareholder of the South Indian Bank holding 11.25 percent of the bank's equity. South Indian Bank has several firsts to its credit.

1. First among the private sector banks in Kerala to become a scheduled bank in 1946 under the RBI Act.
2. First bank in the private sector in India to open a currency chest on behalf of the RBI in April 1992.
3. First private sector bank to open a NRI branch in November 1992.
4. First bank in the private sector to start an industrial finance branch in March 1993.
5. First among the private sector banks in Kerala to open an "overseas branch" to cater exclusively to the export and import business in June 1993.
6. First bank in Kerala to develop an in-house, a fully integrated branch automation software in addition to the in-house partial automation solution operational since 1992.

The bank had a branch network of 403 and an ATM network of 605 as on September 30, 2011. Presently, South Indian Bank has a network of 450 branches and 45 extension counters spread over 19 States/UT.

**6.7 City Union Bank Ltd.**

The bank, 'The Kumbakonam Bank Limited' as it was then called was incorporated as a limited company on 31st October, 1904.

The first memorandum of association was signed by twenty devoted and prominent citizens of Kumbakonam including Sarvashri R. Santhanam Iyer, S. Krishna Iyer, V. Krishnaswami Iyengar and T.S. Raghavachariar. T. S. Raghavachariar was the first agent of the bank.

In 1908, he was succeeded by Shri R. Santhanam Iyer who became the secretary of the bank under the amended articles of association which created the office of a secretary to be in charge of the bank's management in place of the agent.

He was succeeded by Shri S. Mahalinga Iyer as secretary who subsequently became the first full-time managing director of the bank in tune with the amendment of Articles in 1929.

He held the position of secretary from 1926 to 1929 and that of managing director from 1929 to 1963. The bank in the beginning preferred the role of a regional bank and slowly but steadily built for itself a place in the Delta district, Thanjavur. The first branch of the bank was opened at Mannargudi on 24th January 1930.

Thereafter, branches were opened at Nagapattinam, Sannanallur, Ayyampet, Tirukattupalli, Tiruvarur, Manapparai, Mayuram and Porayar within a span of twenty five years.

The bank was included in the second schedule of Reserve Bank of India Act, 1934, on March 22, 1945. The bank celebrated its golden jubilee on November 14, 1954 at Kumbakonam. In 1957, the bank took over the assets and liabilities of the Common Wealth Bank Limited and in the process annexed to it the five branches of Common Wealth Bank Limited at Aduthurai, Kodavasal, Valangaiman, Jayankondacholopuram and Ariyalur. In 1963, Shri R.A. Venkataramani Iyer took charge as the chairman of the bank which position he held up to 1969. In April, 1965, two other local banks viz. 'The City Forward Bank Limited' and 'The Union Bank Limited' were amalgamated with the bank under a scheme of amalgamation with the resultant addition of six more branches viz. Kumbakonam-Town, Nannilam, Koradacherry, Tiruvidaimarudur, Tirupanandal and Kuttalam. Consequently, the bank's name was changed to 'The Kumbakonam City Union Bank Limited'.

In November 1965, the bank's first branch at Madras was opened at Thiyagaraya Nagar. In May, 1969 the bank secured the services of Shri O.R. Srinivasan, a former officer of Reserve Bank of India to be at the helm of affairs as chairman and chief executive officer which event proved to be a turning point in the annals of the bank.

Under the new management the branch expansion got a fresh impetus and branches were opened at Eravancheri, Sembanarkoil, Tiruchirapalli, Madurai, Thanjavur, Dindigul, Keelapalur, Tirumakkottai, Kottur, Tiruvarur Town and Coimbatore during the period from March, 1968 to August, 1973.

During the period 1974-1976, branches were opened at Periyakulam, Mandaveli (Madras), Pattukkottai, Triplicane (Madras), Cuddalore, Pudukkottai, Chidambaram and Salem. The Bank celebrated its platinum jubilee on 9th December, 1979. The first branch outside the State of Tamil Nadu was opened at Sultanpet, Bengaluru in Karnataka in September, 1980. Branches were also opened at the twin cities of Hyderabad and Secunderabad in Andhra Pradesh. In tune with the national image attached to the bank, the bank's name was changed to 'City Union Bank Limited' with effect from December, 1987. The bank started its own staff training college on August 21, 1989 at Kumbakonam.

The bank obtained license from Insurance Regulatory Authority of India (IRDA) to act as corporate agent for selling insurance products and to provide value added services to the public at large. The bank entered into memoranda of understanding with Life Insurance Corporation of India and National Insurance Company Limited for selling their insurance products. The bank has entered into a franchise agreement for the money transfer service scheme of UAE Exchange and Financial Service Ltd., ICICI, Doha Bank and Bank of India for effective and speedy receipt of funds remitted from abroad. The bank has obtained license to function as depository participant under National Securities Depository Limited. The bank's centenary celebrations were inaugurated on December 27, 2003 at the Saraswathi Patasala Girl's Higher Secondary School Grounds, Kumbakonam. The bank presently has 286 branches.

**6.8 ING Vysya Bank Ltd.**

ING Vysya Bank Ltd., is an entity formed with the coming together of erstwhile, Vysya Bank Ltd., a premier bank in the Indian private sector and a global financial powerhouse, ING of Dutch origin, during October 2002. The origin of the erstwhile Vysya Bank was pretty humble.

It was in the year 1930 that a team of visionaries came together to form a bank that would extend a helping hand to those who weren't privileged enough to enjoy Banking services. In 1980, the bank completed fifty years of service to the nation and post 1985, the bank made rapid strides to reach the coveted position of being the number one private sector bank. In 1990, the bank completed its diamond jubilee year. The 75th anniversary, the platinum jubilee of the bank was celebrated during 2005.

The long journey of seventy-five years has had several milestones:

1. 1930—set up in Bengaluru.
2. 1948—scheduled bank.
3. 1985—largest private sector bank.
4. 1987—The Vysya Bank Leasing Ltd. commenced.
5. 1990—promoted Vysya Bank Housing Finance Ltd.
6. Cash management services and commissioning of VSAT.

Golden Peacock Award for the best HR practices by Institute of Directors. Rated as best domestic bank in India by Global Finance (International Financial Journal-June 1998).

7. 2001—ING-Vysya commenced life insurance business.
8. 2002—ING takes over the management of the bank from 7th October 2002.
9. RBI clears the new name of the bank as ING Vysya Bank Ltd.

**6.9 Tamilnad Mercantile Bank Limited**

The history of Tamilnad Mercantile Bank Ltd., the then Nadar Bank Ltd., dates back to 1921. The thought of establishing a bank under the guidance of the able Nadar business community was mooted out in the anniversary of Nadar Mahajana Sangam held at Tuticorin in 1920. The proposal was effected soon and the bank was registered on May 11, 1921 as "The Nadar Bank Ltd.". A group of dedicated men with shrewd acumen and sound integrity were constituted as board of directors and they elected Shri M.V. Shanmugavel Nadar as chairman on November 4, 1921. The bank was opened by Shri T.V. Balagurusamy Nadar, the then president of the Nadar Mahajana Sangam and the bank threw open its door to the public on 11th November, 1921 in Ana Mavanna Building at South Raja Street, Tuticorin. The bank was having only 4 branches until the year 1947 at Tuticorin, Madurai, Sivakasi and Virudhunagar.

The bank had also a branch at Colombo in the year 1937 and the same was closed in the year 1939. The first branch outside the state of Tamil Nadu was opened in the year 1976 at Bengaluru. The first fully computerized branch was opened at WGC Road, Tuticorin on December 9, 1984. The bank established its first currency chest in 1993 at Madurai and has industrial finance branches at Coimbatore, Chennai and Secunderabad. The bank launched ATM card from 11th November 2003. The bank has now 285 full fledged branches all over India and tie-up arrangements with HDFC Bank (531 locations) and IDBI Bank (136 locations) gives an effective branch network of 930. All the 285 branches are computerised and inter-connected. Out of 285 branches, 219 branches are located at rural, semi urban and urban (non-metro) centres.

The bank which had a deposit base of ₹ 21,010 in the year 1921 increased it to ₹ 27 lakh during 1946 and to ₹ 182 lakh during 1971. Deposit level of the bank as on March 31, 2012 was ₹ 17,137 crore, which pronounces the confidence of the public reposed on the bank. The level of advances which stood at ₹ 52 Lakh in the year 1962 has spurted to above ₹ 13,897 crore now. Tamilnad Mercantile Bank Ltd., is the only bank in India declaring consistently higher rate of dividend to its shareholders from the very beginning. The bank had declared 6 percent dividend to its shareholders in 1921. The rate of dividend has been on increasing trend. The bank declared a dividend of 1000 percent for each of the financial year ended on March 31, 2006 and 2007. The bank, which had a net profit of ₹ 6,984 in the year 1921 had spurted to ₹ 5.05 lakh in the year 1971 and to ₹ 313.46 crore for the year ended March 2012. The bank's board of directors recommended a dividend of ₹ 1,000 a share of ₹ 10 each in 2010-11. This is a record 10,000 percent dividend.

The official motto of the Bank is "Totally Motivated Bank".

## 6.10 Jammu and Kashmir Bank

Jammu and Kashmir Bank is the only bank in the country with majority ownership vested with a state government–the Government of Jammu & Kashmir. J&K Bank functions as a universal bank in Jammu & Kashmir and as a specialised bank in the rest of the country. It is also the only private sector bank designated as RBI's agent for banking business, and carries out the banking business of the Central Government, besides collecting central taxes for CBDT. J&K Bank follows a two-legged business model whereby it seeks to increase lending in its home state which results in higher margins despite modest volumes, and at the same time, seeks to capture niche lending opportunities on a pan-India basis to build volumes and improve margins. J&K Bank operates on the principle of 'socially empowering Banking' and seeks to deliver innovative financial solutions for household, small and medium enterprises.

The bank, incorporated in 1938, is listed on the NSE and the BSE. It has a track record of uninterrupted profits and dividends for four decades. The J&K Bank is rated P1+, indicating the highest degree of safety by Standard & Poor and CRISIL.

### 6.11 Lakshmi Vilas Bank

The Lakshmi Vilas Bank Limited (LVB) was founded eight decades ago, in 1926 by seven people of Karur under the leadership of Shri V.S.N. Ramalinga Chettiar, mainly to cater to the financial needs of varied customer segments. The bank was incorporated on 3rd November, 1926 under the Indian Companies Act, 1913 and obtained the certificate to commence business on November 10, 1926. It obtained license from RBI in June 1958 and in August 1958 it became a scheduled commercial bank. During 1961-65, LVB took over nine banks and raised its branch network considerably. To meet the emerging challenges in the competitive business world, the bank started expanded its boundaries beyond Tamil Nadu from 1974 by opening branches in the states of Andhra Pradesh, Karnataka, Kerala, Maharashtra, Madhya Pradesh, Gujarat, West Bengal, Uttar Pradesh, Delhi and Pondicherry. At present it has a network of 276 branches,1 satellite branch and 9 extension counters, spread over 15 states and the union territory of Puducherry. LVB has been focusing on retail banking, corporate banking and bancassurance. The bank has an ATM network of 502, in vital/major locations.

To facilitate all the financial services under one roof, the bank has tied up for a bancassurance pact with Life Insurance

Corporation of India for marketing life insurance products, Bajaj Allianz General Insurance Co. Ltd for general insurance distribution business and arrangements for distributing the mutual fund products of 16 various reputed AMCs.

## 6.12 The Nainital Bank Limited

The Nainital Bank Limited (NBL) (known as Nainital Bank) is a private Indian bank, established in 1954. Nainital Bank was founded by Govind Ballabh Pant and a few other prominent men from the Shah/Sah community of Kumaon. Based in Nainital, over the years, the bank has expanded in Uttar Pradesh and Uttarakhand State, and has over 100 branches in Rajasthan, Delhi and Haryana states. In 1975, Government-owned Bank of Baroda (BOB), the third largest bank in India acquired a majority stake (98.6 percent) and management control of the bank, and made it a subsidiary. Today, it is registered as a scheduled commercial bank with the Reserve Bank of India.

In April, 2004, National Insurance Company (NIC) signed an agreement with Nainital Bank for distribution of its general insurance products through the bank's branches across Uttarakhand, Haryana and New Delhi states. The bank launched its rights issue in September 2009, to expand its capital adequacy ratio (CAR) after it previously withdrew its plans for an IPO due to adverse market conditions in 2007.

Nainital Bank is associated with Bank of Baroda, HDFC Bank, LIC, National Insurance Company Limited etc.

## 6.13 Ratnakar Bank

Inspired by the call for self-reliance given by national leaders in the pre-Independence era, a group of patriotic, eminent personalities from various walks of life came together to launch a crusade for economic independence. The Ratnakar Bank was established in the year 1943 in the month of August by the driving force of Shri Babgonda Bhujgonda Patil, a distinguished Advocate of Sangli and Shri Gangaram

Siddhappa Chougule, a renowned merchant of Kolhapur. In the year 1956, the bank was conferred the rank of scheduled commercial bank by the Reserve Bank of India. Ever since its establishment, the bank has been serving its customers with excellent services and facilities.

The core mission of Ratnakar Bank is:

"To develop a professional and managed platform based on relationships, knowledge, sector expertise and technology to:

1. Build a customer-centric retail banking business.
2. Identify and partner with SME's and emerging local corporates with outstanding business models, providing them a full range of financial services so as to enable them to become world-class enterprises.
3. Deliver robust and cost-effective banking services that promote financial Inclusion, catalyze growth and reduce social inequalities".

The goal of Ratnakar Bank is to be the 'Bank of Choice' in its selected client and geographic segments.

### 6.14 Bank of Rajasthan

A leading private sector bank, the Bank of Rajasthan was founded on the auspicious day of Akshya Tritiya on May 8, 1943, at Udaipur. Shri Rai Bahadur P.C. Chatterji, the then finance minister of the erstwhile Mewar Government, extensively contributed towards the establishment of the bank. The bank started with a capital of only ₹ 10 lakh. Late Seth Shri Govind Ram Seksaria, an eminent industrialist, was the founder chairman. It was, in 1948, that the Bank of Rajasthan became a scheduled bank. Bank of Rajasthan was one among the first banks to take banking services, to the door step of customers.

This was done, when it opened its first mobile branch in Jaipur on August 5, 1960, thereby initiating the concept of mobile branches. The bank became one of the earliest banks in private sector sponsoring any rural (Gramin) bank, when it established the Mewar Anchlik Gramin Bank in Udaipur District in Rajasthan on January 26, 1983. Further in 1997, the bank achieved distinction, when its Jaipur branch qualified for ISO 9002: 94 certification by Det Norske Veritas (DNV), London. The Reserve Bank of India approved the merger of Bank of Rajasthan with ICICI Bank Ltd., India's largest private sector bank. All branches of Bank of Rajasthan now function as branches of ICICI Bank. The boards of both the banks on May 23, 2010 approved the merger for a share exchange ratio of 25 shares of ICICI Bank for 118 shares of Bank of Rajasthan.

To sum up, the fast-changing banking landscape in the country has made old generation private sector banks sit up and chart an image makeover plan. More and more such banks, including smaller lenders like Lakshmi Vilas Bank (LVB), Karur Vysya Bank (KVB), Karnataka Bank (KB), Tamilnad Mercantile Bank (TMB) and South Indian Bank, are roping in executives from foreign and new generation private sector counterparts to help them not only in brand building but also expanding out of their traditional pockets. In addition, they are also diversifying into new business and mulling stake sale to raise funds for expansion.

LVB recently applied to the Reserve Bank to spin off a housing finance company. It is also mulling a dilution of equity stake of up to 40 percent of the present capital by way of qualified institutional placement (QIP), GDR/GDRs or even a follow-on public offer (FPO). Karur-based KVB appointed Boston Consultancy recently to chart out a road map for attaining the targets and position itself to face competition from new generation banks. Tamilnad Mercantile Bank (TMB) is currently considering a re-branding exercise to increase its visibility. By 2013, it aims to expand beyond South India and to attain a total business of ₹ 50,000 crore with 500 branches going beyond South. As on March 2011, its total business was at ₹ 24,679 crore.

Meanwhile, the market buzz is that these small lenders

could be taken over by the larger banks. Market analysts say claiming higher valuations could be one of the reasons behind the expansion of these banks.

# 7

# New Generation Private Sector Banks

The nationalization of major banks in India occurred on 19th July 1969. The Government of India (GoI) issued an ordinance and nationalized the 14 largest commercial banks of India, including Punjab National Bank (PNB), Allahabad Bank, Canara Bank, Central Bank of India, etc. Public sector banks were revived to take up leading role in the banking structure. In 1980, the GoI nationalized 6 more commercial banks, getting control over 91 percent of banking business of India.

In 1994, the Reserve Bank of India issued a policy of liberalization to license limited number of private banks, which came to be known as new generation private sector banks. Global Trust Bank was the first private bank to be established after liberalization. It was later amalgamated with Oriental Bank of Commerce (OBC). Housing Development Finance Corporation Limited (HDFC) became the first (still existing) to receive an 'in principle' approval from the Reserve Bank of India (RBI) to set up a bank in the private sector.

At present, new generation private banks in India include leading Banks like ICICI Bank, HDFC Bank, Yes Bank, IndusInd Bank, Kotak Mahindra Bank, Development Credit Bank, etc. Undoubtedly, being tech-savvy and full of expertise, private banks have played a major role in the development of Indian banking industry. They have made banking more efficient and customer friendly. In the process, they have jolted public sector banks out of complacency and forced them to become more competitive.

## 7.1 Axis Bank Ltd.

Axis Bank was formed as UTI Bank when it was incorporated in 1994 after Government of India allowed private players in the banking sector. Axis Bank was the first of the new private banks to begin operations in 1994. The bank was sponsored together by the administrator of the specified undertaking of the Unit Trust of India, Life Insurance Corporation of India and General Insurance Corporation Ltd. and its subsidiaries namely National Insurance Company Ltd., the New India Assurance Company, the Oriental Insurance Company and United Insurance Company Ltd.

The name of UTI Bank was changed because of the disagreement on terms and conditions of the bank authority over certain stipulations including royalty charged over the name from UTI AMC. The bank also wanted to have a new name from its pan-Indian as well as international business perspective. So from July 30, 2007 onwards the UTI Bank was named as Axis Bank.

Axis Bank Ltd. was promoted by the largest financial institution of the country, UTI. The bank was set up with a capital of ₹ 115 crore, with UTI contributing ₹ 100 crore, LIC ₹ 7.5 crore and GIC and its four subsidiaries contributing ₹ 1.5 crore each. The bank has strengths in both retail and corporate banking and is committed to adopting the best industry practices internationally in order to achieve excellence.

Axis Bank Foundation (ABF) was setup as a public trust in 2006 to carry out the corporate social responsibility initiatives of Axis Bank. ABF has partnered with several NGOs to provide equitable education to various underprivileged individuals across 13 states of India.

In 2011, ABF ventured into the domain of providing sustainable livelihood and aims at alleviating poverty and providing livelihood options for economically weak households. It also aims to help create capabilities in terms of skills and employment opportunities for disadvantaged/differently-abled people especially children.

Besides the philanthropic initiatives of ABF, it has also setup a volunteering program, encouraging employees of the bank to get involved and become socially responsible citizens.

ABF is actively involved in making steps towards reversing the effects of our ecological footprints, by implementing several sustainability initiatives. Philosophy of Axis Bank Foundation is to strive to improve the standard of living of the underprivileged people in India, by providing them education, healthcare and livelihoods.

Since 2006, ABF has supported 74 NGOs located in 15 states of India. Its initiatives in education have been able to directly impact over 88,000 individuals through 9 sustainable livelihood initiatives that have been launched, impacting the lives of around 4.5 lakh families,

Through its highway trauma care initiative it has assisted 7124 major accident victims and around 15,000 minor accident victims.

ABF has implemented a recycling programme under which all the dry waste is converted into eco-friendly notebooks and notepads.

### 7.2 Development Credit Bank Limited

DCB was converted into a scheduled commercial bank on 31st May 1995, in the wake of India's economic liberalization. It was the only cooperative bank, which successfully crossed over and thrived in the face of change. It was founded in the 1930s in Mumbai from a series of cooperative bank mergers with the Ismailia Cooperative Bank Limited and the Masalawala Cooperative Bank. These 2 banks later merged to form Development Cooperative Bank, which was changed to Development Credit Bank after it was granted the scheduled bank license by the Reserve Bank of India on May 31, 1995. The bank went on to successfully offer shares to the public by an initial public offering (IPO) in 2006. The Aga Khan Fund for Economic Development (AKFED) is the largest stakeholder in the bank with around 23 percent stake. Public shareholding under the resident individual category is approximately 39.4 percent. The bank has a network of 82 state-of-the-art, customer friendly, and conveniently located branches across the states of Maharashtra, Gujarat, Andhra Pradesh, Karnataka, Delhi/NCR, Rajasthan, Goa, Tamil Nadu, Haryana, West Bengal and the Union Territories of Daman and Diu and Dadra and Nagar Haveli.

To adhere to its vision of attaining the gold standard in customer service in Indian banking, intensive training and service quality programmes have been initiated with customer delight becoming the key focus of the bank.

**7.3 HDFC Bank Limited**

The Housing Development Finance Corporation Limited (HDFC) was amongst the first to receive an 'in principle' approval from the Reserve Bank of India (RBI) to set up a bank in the private sector, as part of the RBI's liberalisation of the Indian banking Industry in 1994. The bank was incorporated in August 1994 in the name of 'HDFC Bank Limited', with its registered office in Mumbai, India. HDFC Bank commenced operations as a scheduled commercial bank in January 1995.

HDFC is India's premier housing finance company and enjoys an impeccable track record in India as well as in international markets. Since its inception in 1977, the corporation has maintained a consistent and healthy growth in its operations to remain the market leader in mortgages. Its outstanding loan portfolio covers well over a million dwelling units. HDFC has developed significant expertise in retail mortgage loans to different market segments and also has a large corporate client base for its housing related credit facilities. With its experience in the financial markets, a strong market reputation, large shareholder base and unique consumer franchise, HDFC was ideally positioned to promote a bank in the Indian environment.

In 2002, Times Bank Limited, a private sector bank promoted by Bennett, Coleman and Co. (Times Group) was merged with HDFC Bank. With this, HDFC and Times became the first two private banks in the new generation private sector banks to have gone through a merger. In 2008, RBI approved the amalgamation of Centurion Bank of Punjab with HDFC Bank. The deposits of the merged entity became ₹ 1,22,000 crore, while the advances were ₹ 89,000 crore.

At present, HDFC Bank has an authorized capital of ₹ 550 crore, of this the paid-up amount is ₹ 424.6 crore. In terms of equity share, the HDFC Group holds 19.4 percent, foreign institutional investors (FIIs) have around 28 percent of the equity and about 17.6 percent is held by the ADS Depository [the Bank's American Depository Shares (ADS) Issue].

The bank has about 5,70,000 shareholders. Its shares find a listing on the Bombay Stock Exchange and National Stock Exchange, while its American Depository Shares are listed on the New York Stock Exchange (NYSE), under the symbol 'HDB'.

HDFC Bank began operations in 1995 with a simple mission: To be a "world-class Indian bank". It realised that only a single-minded focus on product quality and service excellence would help them get there.

## 7.4 ICICI Bank Limited

ICICI Bank started as a wholly owned subsidiary of ICICI Limited, an Indian financial institution, in 1994. Four years later, when the company offered ICICI Bank shares to the public, ICICI's shareholding was reduced to 46 percent. In the year 2000, ICICI Bank offered an equity offering in the form of ADRs on the New York Stock Exchange (NYSE), thereby becoming the first Indian company and the first bank or financial institution from non-Japan Asia to be listed on the NYSE. In the next year, it acquired the Bank of Madura Limited.

With a change in the corporate structure and the budding competition in the Indian banking industry, the management of both ICICI and ICICI Bank were of the opinion that a merger between the two entities would prove to be an essential step. It was in 2001 that the boards of directors of ICICI and ICICI

Bank sanctioned the amalgamation of ICICI and two of its wholly-owned retail finance subsidiaries, ICICI Personal Financial Services Limited and ICICI Capital Services Limited, with ICICI Bank. In the following year, the merger was approved by its shareholders, the High Court of Gujarat at Ahmedabad as well as the High Court of Judicature at Mumbai and the Reserve Bank of India.

ICICI Bank is India's second-largest bank with total assets of ₹ 47,365 crore as on March 31, 2012 and profit after tax ₹ 6,465 crore for the year ended March 31, 2012. The bank has a network of 2,766 branches and about 9,363 ATMs in India, and has a presence in 19 countries, including India. The bank currently has subsidiaries in the United Kingdom, Russia and Canada, branches in United States, Singapore, Bahrain, Hong Kong, Sri Lanka, Qatar and Dubai International Finance Centre and representative offices in United Arab Emirates, China, South Africa, Bangladesh, Thailand, Malaysia and Indonesia.

For over five decades, the ICICI Group has partnered India in its economic growth and development. Promoting inclusive growth has been a priority area for the Group from both a social and business perspective. ICICI Group strives to make a difference to its customers, to the society and to the nation's development directly through its products and services, as well as through development initiatives and community outreach.

ICICI Foundation for Inclusive Growth (ICICI Foundation) was founded by the ICICI Group in early 2008 to carry forward and build upon its legacy of promoting inclusive growth. ICICI Foundation works within public systems and specialised grassroots organisations to support developmental work. The foundation is committed to investing in long-term efforts to support inclusive growth through effective interventions.

Its vision is a world free of poverty in which every individual has the freedom and power to create and sustain a just society in which to live.

ICICI Bank's Social Initiatives Group (SIG), a non-profit group set up within ICICI Bank in 2000, pioneered work on primary health, elementary education and access to finance. In January 2008, ICICI Group established ICICI Foundation for inclusive growth, which carries forward this legacy.

**7.5 IndusInd Bank Ltd.**

IndusInd Bank, which commenced its operations in 1994, caters to the needs of both consumer and corporate customers. It has a robust technology platform supporting multi-channel delivery capabilities.

IndusInd Bank derives its name and inspiration from the Indus Valley civilization—a culture described by National Geographic as 'one of the greatest of the ancient world' combining a spirit of innovation with sound business and trade practices.

Mr. Srichand P. Hinduja, a leading non-resident Indian businessman and head of the Hinduja Group, conceived the vision of IndusInd Bank and through collective contributions from the NRI community towards India's economic and social development, brought the bank into being.

The bank was formally inaugurated in April 1994 by Dr. Manmohan Singh, Honourable Prime Minister of India who was then the country's finance minister.

It started with a capital base of ₹ 100 crore, of which ₹ 60 crore was raised through private placement from Indian Residents while the balance ₹ 40 crore was contributed by non-resident Indians. It was established with the help of collective contributions from the NRI community, towards the economic and social development of India. A decade after its establishment i.e. in June 2004, IndusInd Bank was merged with Ashok Leyland Finance Ltd., which was one of the largest leasing finance and hire purchase companies in India, at that time. With this, the bank increased its customer base and geographical penetration.

Within a few years of its foundation, IndusInd Bank

started climbing the ladder of success and became one of the fastest-growing banks in the Indian banking sector. By 2006, it had expanded its branch network, from 61 in 2004, to 137. Apart from setting up 150 ATM centres of its own, the bank also concluded multilateral arrangements with other banks, taking the total number of authorized ATM outlets to 15,000.

### 7.6 Kotak Mahindra Bank Limited

Kotak Mahindra Bank is one of India's leading financial private banking institutions. It offers banking solutions that covers almost every sphere of life. Some of its financial services include commercial banking, stock broking, mutual funds, life insurance and investment banking. Established under the brand of Kotak Mahindra Finance Ltd. in 1984, it was given the license to carry on with banking business by the Reserve Bank of India in February 2003. It is the first company in the Indian banking history to be converted from a private financial institution to a bank.

Within a small span of 9 years, the bank has spread its wings in several sphere of finances. Presently, spread in 82 cities in India, the bank caters to the needs of its 59 lakh customers spread throughout the length and breadth of country and even abroad. The entire Kotak Mahindra group has a net worth of over ₹ 6,327 crore and at the end of FY 2007-2008, it was reported that the consolidated profit of Kotak Mahindra Bank individually was ₹ 991.2 crore which was 84 percent higher than the consolidated profit of ₹ 538.2 crore in FY 2006-2007. Kotak Mahindra Bank has 75 ATMs at 41 locations in the country which are 24x7 accessible. Before the free transactions facility of RBI was made mandatory to all the ATM operating banks in India from April 1, 2009, Kotak Mahindra Bank had entered into a treaty with the HDFC Bank to provide access to the ATM network free of cost to most of its customers through its 1335 ATMs spread in the country to ensure comfort to its customers.

### 7.7 Yes Bank

Yes Bank was established and is run by Rana Kapoor and Ashok Kapur with the financial support of Rabo Bank Nederland, the world's single AAA rated private bank. Three respected global institutional private equity investors, CVC Citigroup, AIF Capital and Chrys Capital are also associated with this bank. Yes Bank was established with the motto of providing Indian customers a spirit of professional entrepreneurship blended with a premium quality service and technologically savvy banking trends. Yes Bank has been recently rated to be the second best private bank in India on its overall performance. The bank is spread in India with a total of 117 branches in India most of which are located in north India. The biggest feature that differentiates the standard of Yes Bank from a mediocre bank is the inclusion of knowledge bankers in its management team, who have an expertise in the Indian economy. This expertise proves beneficial to the customers of the bank. Apart from this, the philosophy of technological edge, corporate governance and responsible banking also sets a standard set of working parameters for the bank.

The bank as per its motto of technological advancement is also well equipped with the modern day amenities like net banking, phone banking and mobile banking.

# 8

# Regional Rural Banks (RRBs)

## 8.1 Introduction

The institution of regional rural banks (RRBs) was created to meet the excess demand for institutional credit in the rural areas, particularly among the economically and socially marginalised sections. Although the cooperative banks and the commercial banks had reasonable records in terms of geographical coverage and disbursement of credit, in terms of population groups the cooperative banks were dominated by the rural rich, while the commercial banks had a clear urban bias. In order to provide access to low-cost banking facilities to the poor, the Narasimham Working Group (1975) proposed the establishment of a new set of banks, as institutions which "combine the local feel and the familiarity with rural problems which the cooperatives possess and the degree of business organization, ability to mobilize deposits, access to central money markets and modernized outlook which the commercial banks have".

The Narsimham Committee conceptualized the creation of RRBs in 1975 as a new set of regionally-oriented rural banks, which would combine the local feel and familiarity of rural problems characteristic of cooperatives with the professionalism and large resource base of commercial banks. Regional rural banks were established under the provisions of an Ordinance promulgated on the September 26, 1975 and the RRB Act, 1976. Their equity is held by the Central Government, State Government concerned and the Sponsor Bank in the proportion of 50:15:35. RRBs were supposed to evolve as specialised rural financial institutions for developing the rural economy by providing credit to small and marginal farmers, agricultural labourers, artisans and small entrepreneurs.

The multi-agency approach to rural credit was also to subserve the needs of the input-intensive agricultural strategy (Green Revolution) which had initially focused on "betting on the strong" but by the mid-seventies was ready to spread more widely through the Indian countryside. In addition, the potential and need for diversification of economic activities in the rural areas had begun to be recognized, and this was a sector where the RRBs could play a meaningful role. The RRBs Act, 1976 sums up this overall vision to sub-serve both the developmental and the redistributive objectives: "The RRBs were established with a view to developing the rural economy by providing, for the purpose of development of agriculture, trade, commerce, industry and other productive activities in the rural areas, credit and other facilities, particularly to small and marginal farmers, agricultural labourers, artisans and small entrepreneurs, and for matters connected therewith and incidental thereto".

The RRBs mobilize financial resources from rural/semi-urban areas and grant loans and advances mostly to small and marginal farmers, agricultural labourers and rural artisans. The area of operation of RRBs is limited to the area as notified by GoI covering one or more districts in the State.

In the year 1989 for the first time, the conceptualization of the entire structure of regional rural banks was challenged by the Agricultural Credit Review Committee (Khusro Committee), which argued that these banks have no justifiable cause for continuance and recommended their mergers with sponsor banks. The Committee was of the view that "the weaknesses of RRBs are endemic to the system and non-viability is built into it, and the only option was to merge the RRBs with the sponsor banks. The objective of serving the weaker sections effectively could be achieved only by self-sustaining credit institutions". At the time such a policy move was politically unthinkable, so the Reserve Bank and the Government of India quite prudently pushed the Khusro

Committee report under the carpet without a public debate.

With the onset of the neo-liberal economic reforms and the liberalization of the financial system, the RRBs came under the scanner once again, but this time in a policy regime that was too willing to let the market principles rule. The Committee on Financial Systems, 1991 (Narasimham Committee) stressed the poor financial health of the RRBs to the exclusion of every other performance indicator. 172 of the 196 RRBs were unprofitable with an aggregate loan recovery performance of 40.8 percent (June 1993). The low equity base of these Banks (paid up capital of ₹ 25 lakh) didn't cover for the loan losses of most RRBs.

In the case of a few RRBs, there had also been an erosion of public deposits, besides capital. In order to impart viability to the operations of RRBs, the Narasimham Committee suggested that the RRBs should be permitted to engage in all types of banking business and should not be forced to restrict their operations to the target groups, a proposal which was readily accepted. This recommendation marked a major turning point in the functioning of RRBs as we shall see below. For the time being though, the suggestion of mergers of the RRBs with their sponsor bank, which the Committee on Financial Systems had put forth in a slightly modified form, "sponsor banks might decide whether to retain the identities of sponsored RRBs or to merge them with rural subsidiaries of commercial Banks to be set up on the recommendation of the committee" was put on hold.

In the ensuing years, reforms of the RRBs largely followed the same format as that of the commercial banks, irrespective of the fact that their very role in the society required a special status and a different set of policies. Since the early 1990s, there was a complete freeze on recruitment of new staff in the RRBs. As a part of comprehensive restructuring programme, recapitalisation of the RRBs was initiated in the year 1994-95, a process which continued till 1999-2000 and covered 187 RRBs with aggregate financial support of ₹ 2188.44 crore from the stakeholders. Simultaneously, prudential norms on income-recognition, asset classification and provisioning for loan-losses following customary banking benchmarks were introduced. Since 1996-97, there has been a tendency to allow greater role and larger operational responsibilities to sponsor banks in the management of RRBs.

RRBs started their development process on October 2, 1975 with the formation of a single bank (Prathama Grameen Bank). As on March 31, 2006, there were 133 RRBs (post-merger) covering 525 districts with a network of 14,494 branches. RRBs were originally conceived as low cost institutions having a rural ethos, local feel and pro poor focus. However, within a very short time, most banks were making losses. The original assumptions as to the low cost nature of these institutions were belied.

When the reform process in the banking sector was initiated, RRBs were taken up for a close look. The GoI in consultation with RBI and NABARD started the reform process through a comprehensive package for RRBs including cleansing their balance sheets and recapitalising them. Extant lending restrictions were removed and space and variety available for investment of their surplus funds was expanded. Simultaneously, a number of human resource development and Organisational Development Initiatives (ODI) were taken up by NABARD with funding support of the Swiss Development Corporation (SDC) and with the tools of training and exposure visits, ODI, technology support, computerization and use of IT, system development, etc. for business development and productivity improvement. By end March 2005, there was a remarkable improvement in the financial performance of RRBs as compared to the position prevailing in 1994-95. The number of Banks reporting profits went up to 166 of the 196 RRBs. As on 31st March 2006, of the total 133 RRBs (post-merger), 111 posted profits and 75 of these RRBs were sustainably viable organisations having no accumulated losses as also posting current profits.

GoI initiated the process of structural consolidation of RRBs by amalgamating RRBs sponsored by the same bank within a State as per the recommendations of the Vyas Committee (2004). The amalgamated RRBs were expected to provide better customer service due to better infrastructure, computerization of branches, pooling of experienced work force, common publicity/marketing efforts, etc. and also derive the benefits of a large area of operation, enhanced credit exposure limits and more diverse banking activities. As a result of the amalgamation, the number of RRBs was reduced from 196 to 133 as on March 31, 2006 and to 82 as on March 31, 2012. Thus, under the amalgamation process, 145 RRBs have been amalgamated to form 45 new RRBs.

### 8.2 RRB's Potential Role in Financial Inclusion

Post-merger RRBs represent a powerful instrument for financial inclusion. Their outreach vis-à-vis other scheduled commercial banks particularly in regions and across population groups facing the brunt of financial exclusion is impressive, as observed from an analysis of basic statistical returns of the RBI and indicated in the following paragraphs. With merger infusing the much needed financial strength in RRBs coupled with the local feel and familiarity they command, RRBs are in a unique position to play a decisive role in financial inclusion.

### 8.3 RRBs as Self-help Promotion Institutions (SHPI)

RRBs have not only provided financial services to the SHG-Bank Linkage Programme, but have also played a significant role as SHPIs. As many as 81 RRBs (March 31, 2010) were functioning as SHPIs with grant assistance from NABARD. Non-availability of good NGOs is a matter of concern especially in North-Eastern, Central and Eastern Regions. RRBs can play a vital role as SHPIs in such areas.

RRBs are well positioned to play a major role in financial inclusion particularly in areas/regions with high rates of financial exclusion. RRBs were originally created to cater to neglected sections/areas as they were expected to have sound financial management combined with local feel and familiarity. With the amalgamation of RRBs, they have acquired the critical mass in terms of financial strength to widen and deepen their outreach. With the requisite strength having been developed, RRBs are the best suited vehicles to widen and deepen the process of financial inclusion. However, utmost care must betaken to ensure that in the process of fulfilling the socio-economic objective of financial inclusion, RRBs' do not again fall into the vicious circle of deteriorating financial performance and deviation from their mandate. RRBs may be provided adequate promotional and developmental assistance to contribute substantially to financial inclusion in a way that the business generated out of inclusion efforts add positively to their performance.

### 8.4 Strategic Microfinance Plan with NABARD Support

RRBs have the potential and capability to emerge as niche operators in microfinance. They are playing a major role in the SHG-Bank Linkage Programme especially as SHPIs. It is significant that as an institution they have the expertise and potential to fulfil both the requirements of SHGs—formation plus nurturing and financial service provisions (credit plus). Their dual role has special meaning in areas which face severe financial exclusion and which do not have a sufficient presence of well performing NGOs. However, to upscale the programme to a level where it can really make a visible impact, RRBs need handholding particularly in the areas of training, promotion and development. NABARD helps in providing the required assistance. NABARD assists to prepare a strategic action plan RRB-wise, for promotion and credit linkage of SHGs. RRBs were to form, nurture and credit link at least 3,000 SHGs in all districts covered by them in North-Eastern, Eastern and Central Regions. NABARD is to closely monitor the programme with focus on qualitative aspects.

**8.5 Separate Credit Plan for Excluded Regions**

RRBs operating in predominantly tribal areas and having high levels of exclusion may prepare annual credit plans having a separate component for excluded groups, which would integrate credit provision with promotional assistance such as agricultural services and assistance for the farm and non farm sectors respectively including entrepreneurship development and formation and strengthening of producer's organisations like dairy cooperatives. Refinance and promotional support may be provided by NABARD to RRBs on a large scale for implementation of these credit plans.

**8.6 Computerisation**

With a view to facilitate the seamless integration of RRBs with the main payment system, there is a need to provide computerisation support to them. Banks are eligible for support from the Financial Inclusion Funds on a matching contribution of 50 percent in regard to districts other than tribal districts and 75 percent in case of branches located in tribal districts under the Tribal Sub Plan for technological upgradation.

Further, now that RRBs are being merged and are becoming large size entities, it is necessary that their boards of management are strengthened and powers delegated to them on policy and business operations, viz. introduction of new liability and credit products, investment decisions, improving market orientation in raising and deployment of resources, non-fund based business, career progression, transfer policy etc.

**8.7 NABARD and RRBs**

RRBs with the support of NABARD, GoI, RBI and the sponsor banks, serves as active financial inclusion players especially in areas with high levels of financial exclusion. In order to build up the skills and expertise of the personnel of RRBs, NABARD has played a crucial role since the inception of RRBs. But for the efforts of NABARD and initiative of sponsor banks besides RRB managements themselves in HR development and in implementation of the reform package, the changes in business performance of RRBs would not have been possible. The work could be accomplished by NABARD working in close tandem with GoI and RBI besides the sponsor Banks. NABARD would continue to give special priority to RRBs to train their staff through the training institutions like the Bankers Institute of Rural Development (BIRD) at Lucknow and the regional training colleges at Mangalore and Bolpur, specially set up for meeting the training requirements of RRBs. NABARD is to design suitable training programmes to enable RRBs to meet the challenges in the present environment.

**8.8 Local Area Banks**

The Finance Minister, in his August 1996 Budget, announced the concept of Local Area Banks (LAB) and following this, the RBI issued guidelines and sought applications for setting up LABs. Only 6 LABs were licensed to operate by RBI, of which 4 are currently functioning. Though the overall performance indicators of functioning LABs appear to be healthy, there have been a few instances of LABs having to close down. Keeping in view the inherent potential of LABs, RBI may consider revisiting the same and keep the option open to allow new LABs to come into operation, especially in districts/regions manifesting high levels of exclusion without compromising on regulatory prescriptions. LABs can integrate well with local financial markets and offer a host of financial services including savings, credit, remittances, insurance, etc.

# 9

# Cooperative Banks

## 9.1 Urban Cooperative Banks

The term urban cooperative banks (UCBs), though not formally defined, refers to primary cooperative banks located in urban and semi-urban areas. These banks, till 1996, were allowed to lend money only for non-agricultural purposes. This distinction does not hold today. These banks were traditionally centred around communities, localities, work place groups. They essentially lent to small borrowers and businesses. Today, their scope of operations has widened considerably.

The origins of the urban cooperative banking movement in India can be traced to the close of nineteenth century when, inspired by the success of the experiments related to the cooperative movement in Britain and the cooperative credit movement in Germany such societies were set up in India. Cooperative societies are based on the principles of cooperation, mutual help, democratic decision-making and open membership. Cooperatives represented a new and alternative approach to organisation as against proprietary firms, partnership firms and joint stock companies which represent the dominant form of commercial organisation.

For the cooperative banks in India, cooperatives are organized groups of people and jointly managed and democratically controlled enterprises. They exist to serve their members and depositors and produce better benefits and services for them. Professionalism in cooperative banks reflects the co-existence of high level of skills and standards in performing, duties entrusted to an individual. Cooperative bank needs current and future development in information technology. It is indeed necessary for cooperative banks to devote adequate attention for maximizing their returns on every unit of resources through effective services. Cooperative banks have completed 100 years of existence in India. They play a very important role in the financial system. The cooperative banks in India form an integral part of our money market today. Therefore, a brief resume of their development should be taken into account. The history of cooperative banks goes back to the year 1904. In 1904, the Cooperative Credit Society Act was enacted to encourage cooperative movement in India. But the development of cooperative banks from 1904 to 1951 was the most disappointing one.

**9.1.1 The Beginning:** The first known mutual aid society in India was probably the 'Anyonya Sahakari Mandali' organised in the erstwhile princely State of Baroda in 1889 under the guidance of Vithal Laxman also known as Bhausaheb Kavthekar. Urban cooperative credit societies, in their formative phase came to be organised on a community basis to meet the consumption oriented credit needs of their members. Salary earners' societies inculcating habits of thrift and self-help played a significant role in popularising the movement, especially amongst the middle class as well as organized labour. From its origins then to today, the thrust of UCBs, historically, has been to mobilise savings from the middle and low income urban groups and purvey credit to their members—many of which belonged to weaker sections.

The enactment of Cooperative Credit Societies Act, 1904, however, gave the real impetus to the movement. The first urban cooperative credit society was registered in Canjeevaram (Kanjivaram) in the erstwhile Madras province in October, 1904. Amongst the prominent credit societies were the Pioneer Urban in Bombay (November 11, 1905), the No.1 Military Accounts Mutual Help Cooperative Credit Society in Poona (January 9, 1906), Cosmos in Poona (January 18, 1906), Gokak Urban (February 15, 1906) and Belgaum Pioneer (February 23, 1906) in the Belgaum district, the Kanakavli-Math Cooperative Credit Society and the Varavade Weavers'

Urban Credit Society (March 13, 1906) in the South Ratnagiri (now Sindhudurg) district. The most prominent amongst the early credit societies was the Bombay Urban Cooperative Credit Society, sponsored by Vithaldas Thackersey and Lallubhai Samaldas established on January 23, 1906.

The Cooperative Credit Societies Act, 1904 was amended in 1912, with a view to broad basing it to enable organisation of non-credit societies. The Maclagan Committee of 1915 was appointed to review their performance and suggest measures for strengthening them. The committee observed that such institutions were eminently suited to cater to the needs of the lower and middle income strata of society and would inculcate the principles of banking amongst the middle classes. The committee also felt that the urban cooperative credit movement was more viable than agricultural credit societies. The recommendations of the Committee went a long way in establishing the urban cooperative credit movement in its own right.

The first phase of cooperative bank development was the formation and regulation of cooperative societies. The constitutional reforms which led to the passing of the Government of India Act in 1919 transferred the subject of "cooperation" from Government of India to the Provincial Governments. The Government of Bombay passed the first State Cooperative Societies Act in 1925 "which not only gave the movement, its size and shape but was a pace setter of cooperative activities and stressed the basic concept of thrift, self-help and mutual aid." This marked the beginning of the second phase in the history of cooperative credit institutions.

There was the general realization that urban banks have an important role to play in economic construction. This was asserted by a host of committees. The Indian Central Banking Enquiry Committee (1931) felt that urban banks have a duty to help the small business and middle class people. The Mehta-Bhansali Committee (1939) recommended that those societies which had fulfilled the criteria of banking should be allowed to work as banks and recommended an association for these banks. The Cooperative Planning Committee (1946) went on record to say that urban banks have been the best agencies for small people in whom joint stock banks are not generally interested. The Rural Banking Enquiry Committee (1950), impressed by the low cost of establishment and operations recommended the establishment of such banks even in places smaller than taluka towns.

The real development of cooperative banks took place only after the recommendations of All India Rural Credit Survey Committee (AIRCSC), which were made with the view to fasten the growth of cooperative banks.

The cooperative banks are expected to perform some duties, namely, extend all types of credit facilities to customers in cash and kind, advance consumption loans, extend banking facilities in rural areas, mobilize deposits, supervise the use of loans etc. The needs of cooperative bank are different. They have faced a lot of problems, which has affected the development of cooperative banks. Therefore, it was necessary to study this matter. The first study of urban cooperative banks was taken up by RBI in the year 1958-59.

The Report published in 1961 acknowledged the widespread and financially sound framework of urban cooperative banks; emphasized the need to establish primary urban cooperative banks in new centres and suggested that State Governments lend active support to their development. In 1963, Varde Committee recommended that such banks should be organised at all urban centres with a population of 1 lakh or more and not by any single community or caste. The committee introduced the concept of minimum capital requirement and the criteria of population for defining the urban centre where UCBs were incorporated.

## 9.2 Cooperative Banks: Main Attributes

A cooperative bank is a financial entity which belongs to its members, who are at the same time the owners and the customers of their bank. Cooperative banks are often created by persons belonging to the same local or professional community or sharing a common interest. Cooperative banks generally provide their members with a wide range of banking and financial services (loans, deposits, banking accounts etc.). Cooperative banks differ from stockholder banks by their organization, their goals, their values and their governance.

In most countries, they are supervised and controlled by banking authorities and have to respect prudential banking regulations, which put them at a level playing field with stockholder banks. Depending on countries, this control and supervision can be implemented directly by state entities or delegated to a cooperative federation or central body.

Cooperative banking is retail and commercial banking organized on a cooperative basis. Cooperative banking institutions take deposits and lend money in most parts of the world.

Cooperative banking, includes retail banking, as carried out by credit unions, mutual savings and loan associations, building societies and cooperatives, as well as commercial Banking services provided by manual organizations (such as cooperative federations) to cooperative businesses.

The structure of commercial banking is of branch-banking type; while the cooperative banking structure is a three tier federal one.

1. A state cooperative bank works at the apex level (i.e. works at state level).
2. The central cooperative bank works at the Intermediate Level (i.e. district cooperative banks works at district level).
3. Primary cooperative credit societies at base level (at village level).

Even if cooperative banks organizational rules can vary according to their respective national legislations, cooperative banks share common features as follows:

**9.2.1 Customer-owned Entities**: In a cooperative bank,

the needs of the customers meet the needs of the owners, as cooperative bank members are both. As a consequence, the first aim of a cooperative bank is not to maximize profit but to provide the best possible products and services to its members. Some cooperative banks only operate with their members but most of them also admit non-member clients to benefit from their banking and financial services.

**9.2.2 Democratic Member Control:** Cooperative banks are owned and controlled by their members, who democratically elect the board of directors. Members usually have equal voting rights, according to the cooperative principle of "one person, one vote".

**9.2.3 Profit Allocation:** In a cooperative bank, a significant part of the yearly profit, benefits or surplus is usually allocated to constitute reserves. A part of this profit can also be distributed to the cooperative members, with legal or statutory limitations in most cases. Profit is usually allocated to members either through a patronage dividend, which is related to the use of the cooperative's products and services by each member, or through an interest or a dividend, which is related to the number of shares subscribed by each member.

Cooperative banks are deeply rooted inside local areas and communities. They are involved in local development and contribute to the sustainable development of their communities, as their members and management board usually belong to the communities in which they exercise their activities. By increasing banking access in areas or markets where other banks are less present, farmers in rural areas, middle or low income households in urban areas–cooperative banks reduce banking exclusion and foster the economic ability of millions of people. They play an influential role on the economic growth in the countries in which they work in and increase the efficiency of the international financial system. Their specific form of enterprise, relying on the above mentioned principles of organization, has proven successful both in developed and developing countries.

## 9.3 RBI Policies for Cooperative Banks

The RBI appointed a high power committee in May 1999 under the chairmanship of Shri. K. Madhava Rao, ex-chief secretary, Government of Andhra Pradesh to review the performance of urban cooperative banks (UCBs) and to suggest necessary measures to strengthen this sector. With reference to the terms given to the Committee, the Committee identified five broad objectives:

1. To preserve the cooperative character of UCBs.
2. To protect the depositors' interest.
3. To reduce financial risk.
4. To put in place strong regulatory norms at the entry level to sustain the operational efficiency of UCBs in a competitive environment and evolve measures to strengthen the existing UCB structure particularly in the context of ever increasing number of weak banks.
5. To align urban banking sector with the other segments of banking sector in the context of application of prudential norms and removing the irritants of dual control regime.
6. RBI has extended the off-site surveillance system (OSS) to all non-scheduled urban cooperative banks (UCBs) having deposit size of ₹ 100 crore and above.

## 9.4 Types of Cooperative Banks

The cooperative banks are small-sized units which operate both in urban and non-urban centres. They finance small borrowers in industrial and trade sectors besides professional and salary classes. Regulated by the Reserve Bank of India, they are governed by the Banking Regulation Act, 1949 and Banking laws (Cooperative Societies) Act, 1965. The cooperative banking structure in India is divided into following components:

**9.4.1 Primary Cooperative Credit Society:** The primary cooperative credit society is an association of borrowers and non-borrowers residing in a particular locality. The funds of the society are derived from the share capital and deposits of members and loans from central cooperative banks. The borrowing powers of the members as well as of the society are fixed. The loans are given to members for the purchase of cattle, fodder, fertilizers, pesticides, etc.

**9.4.2 Central Cooperative Banks:** These are the federations of primary credit societies in a district and are of two types those having a membership of primary societies only and those having a membership of societies as well as individuals. The funds of the bank consist of share capital, deposits, loans and overdrafts from state cooperative banks and joint stocks. These banks provide finance to member societies within the limits of the borrowing capacity of societies. They also conduct all the business of a joint stock bank.

**9.4.3 State Cooperative Banks:** The state cooperative bank is a federation of central cooperative bank and acts as a watchdog of the cooperative banking structure in the state. Its funds are obtained from share capital, deposits, loans and overdrafts from the Reserve Bank of India. The state cooperative banks lend money to central cooperative banks and primary societies and not directly to the farmers.

**9.4.4 Land Development Banks:** The land development banks are organized in 3 tiers namely; state, central, and primary level and they meet the long term credit requirements of the farmers for developmental purposes. The state land development banks oversee, the primary land development banks situated in the districts and tehsil areas in the state. They are governed both by the state government and Reserve Bank of India. Recently, the supervision of land development banks has been assumed by National Bank for Agriculture and Rural Development (NABARD). The sources of funds for these banks are the debentures subscribed by both central and state government. These banks do not accept deposits from the general public.

**9.4.5 Urban Cooperative Banks:** The term urban cooperative banks (UCBs), though not formally defined, refers to primary cooperative banks located in urban and semi-urban areas. These banks, till 1996, were allowed to lend money only for non-agricultural purposes. This distinction does not hold today. These banks were traditionally cantered on communities, localities, work place groups. They essentially lend to small borrowers and businesses. Today, their scope of operations has widened considerably.

## 9.5 Functions of Cooperative Banks

Cooperative banks also perform the basic banking functions but they differ from commercial banks in the following respects:

1. Commercial banks are joint-stock companies under the Companies Act of 1956, or public sector bank under a separate act of a parliament whereas cooperative banks were established under the cooperative societies' acts of different states.
2. Commercial bank structure is branch banking structure whereas cooperative banks have a three tier setup, with state cooperative bank at apex level, central/district cooperative bank at district level, and primary cooperative societies at rural level.
3. Only some of the sections of Banking Regulation Act of 1949 (fully applicable to commercial banks), are applicable to cooperative banks, resulting only in partial control by RBI of cooperative banks.
4. Cooperative banks function on the principle of cooperation and not entirely on commercial parameters.

## 9.6 Concerns Regarding Cooperative Banks

Concerns regarding the professionalism of urban cooperative banks gave rise to the view that they should be better regulated. Large cooperative banks with paid-up share capital and reserves of ₹ 1 lakh were brought under the purview of the Banking Regulation Act, 1949 with effect from 1st March, 1966 and within the ambit of the Reserve Bank's supervision. This marked the beginning of an era of duality of control over these banks. Banking related functions (viz. licensing, area of operations, interest rates etc.) were to be governed by RBI and registration, management, audit and liquidation, etc. governed by State Governments as per the provisions of respective State Acts. In 1968, UCBs were extended the benefits of deposit insurance.

Towards the late 1960s there was debate regarding the promotion of the small scale industries. UCBs came to be seen as important players in this context. The working group on industrial financing through cooperative banks, (1968 known as Damry Group) attempted to broaden the scope of activities of urban cooperative banks by recommending these banks should finance the small and cottage industries.

This was reiterated by the Banking Commission in 1969. The Madhavdas Committee (1979) evaluated the role played by urban cooperative banks in greater details and drew a roadmap for their future role recommending support from RBI and Government in the establishment of such banks in backward areas and prescribing viability standards.

The Hate Working Group (1981) desired better utilization of bank's surplus funds and that the percentage of the cash reserve ratio (CRR) and the statutory liquidity ratio (SLR) of these banks should be brought at par with commercial banks, in a phased manner. While the Marathe Committee (1992) redefined the viability norms and ushered in the era of liberalization, the Madhava Rao Committee (1999) focused on consolidation, control of sickness, better professional standards in urban cooperative banks and sought to align the urban banking movement with commercial banks.

A feature of the urban banking movement has been its heterogeneous character and its uneven geographical spread with most banks concentrated in the states of Gujarat, Karnataka, Maharashtra, and Tamil Nadu. While most banks are unit banks without any branch network, some of the large banks have established their presence in many states when at their behest multi-state banking was allowed in 1985. Some of these banks are also authorized dealers in foreign exchange.

Over the years, primary (urban) cooperative banks have registered a significant growth in number, size and volume of business handled. Recently, the problems faced by a few large UCBs have highlighted some of the difficulties these banks face and policy endeavours are geared to consolidating and strengthening this sector and improving governance.

# 10

# Foreign Banks in India

Foreign banks operating in India are banks of other countries having their branches in India. As on end-June 2011, there were 37 foreign banks operating in India, and 47 foreign banks had their representative offices. After the commencement of business of foreign banks in India, the banking sector in India also become competitive. Foreign banks have brought latest technology and latest banking practices in India. They have helped make Indian banking system more competitive and efficient. Government has come up with a road map for expansion of foreign banks in India.

Foreign banks were established in India quite early during the British rule and have been around for over a century now. As a result of globalization of Indian economy, the number of foreign banks is likely to increase in the coming years. The foreign banks are also called foreign exchange banks, as they also finance the foreign trade of India.

New rules announced by the Reserve Bank of India for the foreign banks in India have put up great hopes among foreign banks which allow them to grow unfettered. Now foreign banks in India are permitted to set up local subsidiaries. The policy conveys that foreign banks in India may not acquire Indian ones (except for weak banks identified by the RBI, on its terms) and their Indian subsidiaries will not be able to open branches freely. During the first phase between March 2005 and March 2009, foreign banks were permitted to establish a presence by way of setting up a wholly-owned subsidiary (WOS) or conversion of existing branches into a WOS.

There is no denying the fact that the foreign banks are playing a pivotal role in the Indian economy. They help the economy by financing the import and export trade of the country. They also receive deposits from the public as fixed deposits and current account deposits. They also give loans and advances to the traders and businessmen. They also issue bank drafts, TTs cheques and mail transfers to the customers. Further, they also help in internal trade, by giving credit facilities to their customers for the procurement of raw materials for transporting goods between manufacturing and trade centres in the country.

Foreign banks have opened up several options for the developing countries to attain economic growth. The achievement of this objective has been made possible partly by foreign exchanges transactions. The advantage is that the foreign banks help finance exports and imports under letter of credit, handling bill business, and by promoting internal trade. In this way they help in earning foreign exchange. As the foreign banks have branches in almost all the other countries of the world, they are able to maintain business links with all those countries for various purposes. These banks help customers to maintain their contacts with their counterparts in other countries.

## 10.1 American Express Bank

American Express was named the 14th most valuable brand in the world by Inter-brand and Business Week in the year 2007, and its total worth was estimated to be around USD 20.87 billion at that time. Owing to the financial crisis in 2008, a Federal Reserve System approval on November 10, 2008 granted conversion of American Express to a bank holding company which led it to receive government help. Fortune ranked American Express as the 62nd best place in the US to work for in the year 2008, which was the top position among the bank card companies in the list. With its headquarters located in New York, US, American Express Company is a global financial services provider, also known as "Amex" in short. American Express had been established in the year 1850, and is well known all around the world for its dedicated credit card, traveller's cheque and charge card services.

American Express Bank is actively present in the Indian market too, with its offices located in Gurgaon (Haryana) and Mathura Road, New Delhi. In India, the services being offered by the American Express Bank primarily are personal and business categories.

**10.2 BNP Paribas**

BNP Paribas is one of the oldest banks in the continent of Europe, and the largest bank in the Eurozone (consortium of countries having adopted Euro as their primary currency), as reported by The Banker magazine. The bank is present in 87 countries with a 162,700 strong workforce offering its services. On the 23rd May 2000, two financial entities viz. the Banque Nationale de Paris (BNP) and Paribas merged together, leading to the formation of the BNP Paribas Bank. BNP Paribas is known as one of the oldest banks of France, along with Crédit Lyonnais (LCL) and Société Générale. BNP Paribas had declared a potential loss of around €350 million due to the Madoff fraud, on the 14th December, 2008.

BNP Paribas has been one of the initial banks to have arrived at the Indian land, and had started its operations in the country as early as year 1860, at Calcutta (now Kolkata). The bank was then known as the Comptoir National d'Escompte de Paris (CNEP). The bank is one of the top corporate banks operating in India, and has now spread its operations to 8 different locations in the country. These locations include Mumbai, New Delhi, Kolkata, Bengaluru, Pune, Ahmedabad, Chennai and Hyderabad.

BNP Paribas carries out a wide range of banking operations in India, which is categorized into three divisions viz. corporate and institutional banking, Private banking and retail banking. In retail banking, the bank provides a range of investment and finance options, such as mutual funds, retail brokerage, home finance and leasing services.

### 10.3 Citibank

Citibank is one of the largest banks in the US, and is a part of the financial services company Citigroup. Citibank was founded in the year 1812. Initially its name was City Bank of New York, which was later changed to First National Citibank of New York. In over 100 countries worldwide, Citibank has been carrying out its operations, which comprise regular banking services along with credit card, insurance and investment services. The bank claims to have a customer base of 15 million users catered by its online services division alone. As Citibank was badly affected by the financial crisis of 2008, the US government provided the bank with an aid of USD 50 billion in two instalments of USD 25 billion each.

In India, Citibank is present at a large number of locations. These locations include Jalandhar, Ludhiana, Chandigarh, Noida, Delhi, Gurgaon, Faridabad, Lucknow, Jaipur, Ahmedabad, Vadodara, Indore, Bhopal, Surat, Nashik, Aurangabad, Akola, Bhubaneswar, Kolkata, Vapi, Mumbai, Pune, Hyderabad, Bengaluru, Chennai, Pondicherry, Cochin and Coimbatore. The bank offers a variety of services and products under the personal banking, NRI banking and corporate banking categories.

Citibank also offers global commercial bank services through its commercial relationship banking wing and global subsidiaries group. The commercial relationship banking services are aimed at helping the small and medium enterprises (SMEs) and mid-market enterprises, while the global subsidiaries group provides comprehensive banking services for the top multinational corporates and their subsidiaries in India.

### 10.4 DBS Bank

DBS Bank is a Singapore-based bank, and is known to be one of the largest banks to exist in South East Asian region by asset value. The government of Singapore established the DBS Bank in the year 1968, and it was primarily aimed at providing development oriented financial services. As of April 2009, the bank is actively operational in 16 markets, and has been listed on the Singapore Exchange (SGX). The bank has "AA-" and "Aa1" credit ratings, which speak for the credibility it enjoys in terms of customer and agency evaluation. The bank has a presence across 200 branches spread across 50 cities, has more than 1,000 ATM installations and 14,000 employees working for it.

Singapore and Hong Kong are the key areas of operation for DBS Bank. Apart from Singapore, DBS Bank has carved out strong presence for itself in China, Hong Kong and Taiwan, collectively known as the Greater China region. DBS Bank was the first Singapore Bank to be incorporated in China in the year 2007, and is present at 12 locations within India as of 2012 with 40 ATMs.

DBS Bank began its operations in India in the year 1994, establishing a representative office in Mumbai, which was converted to a fully operational branch in the month of March 1995. In the year 2005 yet another branch was opened in New Delhi, and in the same year it went into an agreement with Cholamandalam Investments and Finance Company Limited to launch the Cholamandalam DBS Joint Venture. DBS Bank branches are present across many cities in India like Mumbai, Bengaluru, Chennai, Kolkata, New Delhi and Pune. The bank offers a host of banking and financial services to its customers in India, which fall under corporate banking, enterprise banking, financial institution banking and personal banking services comprising of wealth management, NRI services, savings and deposits and DBS Treasures priority banking.

### 10.5 Deutsche Bank

Deutsche Bank was founded in 1870 in Berlin to facilitate trade relations between Germany, other European countries and overseas markets. Today, it has presence in more than 70 countries. Deutsche Bank, headquartered at Frankfurt in Germany, ranks among the global leaders in corporate banking and securities, transaction banking, asset management, and private wealth management. It is one of the world's leading international financial service providers with roughly EURO 2.2 trillion in assets and approximately 80,000 employees. Deutsche Bank is listed on the Frankfurt (FWB) and New York stock exchanges (NYSE).

The bank's business model has two pillars, the Corporate and Investment Bank (CIB) and Private Clients and Asset Management. CIB of Deutsche Bank has established itself as one of the world's leading investment banking houses and is a major contributor in Deutsche Bank's profitability.

Private Clients and Asset Management (PCAM) is comprised of private wealth management, private and business clients and asset management. Private Wealth Management is the bank's private banking arm, serving high net worth individuals.

Deutsche Bank started its operations in India in 1994. Currently, Deutsche Bank operates with staff strength of more than 500 people through its five full-fledged branches in Mumbai, Delhi, Bengaluru, Chennai and Kolkata.

### 10.6 HSBC Bank

HSBC Bank is a subsidiary of HSBC Holdings Plc, a London-based banking giant which, according to the Forbes magazine, is the largest banking group in the world, and the 6th largest company in the world as of April 2009. HSBC Holdings had been established in Hong Kong in the year 1990 as the parent company to the Hong Kong and Shanghai Banking Corporation (HSBC). Further, the bank moved its headquarters from Hong Kong to London.

In India, the introduction of HSBC Bank can be dated as early as the year 1853, with the establishment of the Mercantile Bank of India in Mumbai. Currently, HSBC Group operates through a number of its subsidiaries in India, viz. The Hong Kong and Shanghai Banking Corporation Limited (HSBC), HSBC Asset Management (India) Private Limited,

HSBC Global Resourcing/HSBC Electronic Data Processing (India) Private Limited, HSBC Insurance Brokers (India) Private Limited, HSBC Operations and Processing Enterprise (India) Private Limited, HSBC Private Equity Management (Mauritius) Limited, HSBC Professional Services (India) Private Limited, HSBC Securities and Capital Markets (India) Private Limited and HSBC Software Development (India) Private Limited. The group carries out its commercial banking, banking technology, asset management, global resourcing, insurance and data processing operations in the country through its subsidiaries.

HSBC Bank is well known for having established the first ATM (Automated Teller Machine) in India in the year 1987. As of 31st March, 2011, the bank was present in 50 prominent cities of the country including Mumbai, New Delhi, Bengaluru, Hyderabad, Jaipur, Chandigarh etc. and has 151 ATMs.

## 10.7 Standard Chartered Bank

Standard Chartered Bank is a London-based bank, currently operational in over 70 nations with more than 1,700 branches and 73,000 strong work force. Although the bank is located in Britain, still a huge chunk of its revenues originate from the continents of Asia, Africa and the Middle East. Standard Chartered Bank was formed as the merger of two Banks viz. The Chartered Bank of India, Australia and China and The Standard Bank of British South Africa. The merger took place in the year 1969. Standard Chartered Bank has been actively engaged in acquisitions and expansion, and acquired Grindlays Bank from ANZ Bank in the year 2000 which considerably increased its banking operations in the nations of India and Pakistan. The bank defeated HSBC Bank in a bid to acquire Korea First Bank in the year 2005, which was renamed as SC First Bank after the acquisition. In the year 2006, the bank announced to have acquired an 80 percent stake in the Union Bank of Pakistan for a sum of USD 511 million, making the Standard Chartered Bank (Pakistan) the 6th largest bank in the nation of Pakistan.

In India, the Standard Chartered Bank introduced its first branch in Kolkata on April 12, 1858. Later on, when Mumbai took over Kolkata as the financial capital of India, the bank administration was shifted to Mumbai from Kolkata.

Standard Chartered Bank is located in 94 prominent locations in India, including New Delhi, Mumbai, Kolkata, Bengaluru, Hyderabad, Ahmedabad etc. as on March 31, 2011 and has 319 ATMs.

**10.8 Bank of America**

Bank of America is one of the largest financial service companies in the world. It is the second largest bank in terms of market capitalization. Furthermore, it is the fifth largest company in the United States by total revenue, as well as the second largest non-oil company in the US (after Wal-Mart). In 2010, Bank of America was listed as the 3rd 'best' large company in the world by Forbes. Bank of America has become a major player in the investment banking industry and is one amongst the big four banks of US, after Citigroup, JP Morgan Chase and Wells Fargo. Apart from serving large corporations, Bank of America also serves individual consumers, small and middle market businesses, offering a full range of banking, investing, asset management and other financial products and services.

Bank of America serves clients in 175 countries and has relationships with 99 percent of the US Fortune 500 companies and 83 percent of the Global Fortune 500. The company is a member of the Federal Deposit Insurance Corporation (FDIC) and a component of both the S&P 500 Index and the Dow Jones Industrial Average. Bank of America has approximately 57 million consumer and small business relationships at 5,900 banking centres and 18,000 ATMs. Majority of the bank's services to corporate and institutional clients are provided through its US and UK subsidiaries, Banc of America

Securities LLC and Banc of America Securities Limited.

Bank of America started its commencement of operations in India through its Mumbai branch in 1964. Its headquarters is situated in Mumbai and has five branches across the country in Mumbai, Delhi, Kolkata, Chennai and Bengaluru.

Apart from these major branches, operations of the bank are constantly expanding to cover the entire nation with active support coming from its Indian subsidiaries. Bank of America is strongly making its presence felt in cities like Hyderabad and Gurgaon.

Hyderabad was the first city where Bank of America India operations were initiated and the BPO operations of the bank were further extended to Mumbai. Currently, the BPO operations of Bank of America are mainly operated by the Gurgaon branch office.

Indian subsidiary of the bank, Bank of America Securities Pvt. Ltd. is responsible for operating various activities relating to capital market and fixed income. Another non-bank subsidiary of Bank of America in India is BA Continuum and it offers solutions in areas like business processing, knowledge services and information technology.

## 10.9 The Royal Bank of Scotland

The Royal Bank of Scotland was founded in 1727 and has a history of over three hundred years. With its rich history, it has become one of the largest financial service groups in the world. The headquarters of Royal Bank of Scotland is in Edinburgh, Scotland. The bank is a part of retail banking subsidiaries of the Royal Bank of Scotland Group and along with Nat West and Ulster Bank, provides branch banking facilities in the United Kingdom. The Royal Bank of Scotland and the Royal Bank of Scotland Group are completely separate from the Bank of Scotland, which was established in 1695 and is also based in Edinburgh, Scotland. The Royal Bank of Scotland has around 700 branches, mainly in Scotland. The Royal Bank of Scotland Group provides a strong support to large enterprises, including multi-national corporations (MNC) and financial institutions. In the year 2007, the Royal Bank of Scotland Group strengthened its global presence through purchasing several parts of the Dutch Bank, ABN AMRO, including their businesses in India.

The history of Royal Bank of Scotland in India goes back to 1921. Since then, the bank has expanded significantly across the country, with more than 3,000 staff in Kolkata, Mumbai, New Delhi, Chennai, Pune, Baroda, Hyderabad, Bengaluru, Noida, Gurgaon and Surat branches. There are total of 28 branches throughout the country with 13 lakh customers. The Royal Bank of Scotland's NRI Services provides premium and exclusive banking service to its customers in India. It offers a personalized service based on careful understanding of needs as a non-resident Indian (NRI), helping them before leaving India, while they are abroad and when they plan to return to India. As on March 31, 2011 RBS had 31 branches and 120 ATMs.

### 10.10 UBS Bank

UBS AG is one of the leading Swiss international financial institutes having headquarters in Basel and Zurich, Switzerland. It was founded in 1854 and has a 150 years old heritage. In the year 1998, it got merged with Swiss Bank Corporation. UBS functions in over 40 countries and is regarded as the second largest manager of private wealth assets all over the globe. The bank has numerous offices spread in more than 50 countries with 64,000 employees worldwide. The group's operational structure consists of the corporate centre and four major business divisions, namely Wealth Management & Swiss Bank, Wealth Management Americas, Global Asset Management and the Investment Bank.

UBS is also among the topmost brokers for global investors investing in equities of India. The UBS India Securities Private Ltd.'s brokerage and advisory services can be availed through the bank's India office located in Mumbai which was launched back in 1990. UBS never opted for a joint venture in India and has grown so far by its independent and direct approach strategy. UBS AG opened its branch in Mumbai in 2008. The branch began operating in the following year. As on 31st March, 2011 the Bank had only one branch in India.

### 10.11 Sonali Bank

The largest bank of Bangladesh, Sonali Bank is a state-owned prime and leading commercial bank of the country with its corporate headquarter situated at Motijheel, Dhaka, Bangladesh. Shortly after Bangladesh got Independence, Sonali Bank emanated as the biggest nationalized commercial bank with declaration of the Banks' Nationalization Order, 1972 amalgamating the then National Bank of Pakistan, Premier Bank and Bank of Bhwalpur. When the bank was established, it had a paid up capital of 30 million taka. Sonali Bank has been transformed into a Public Limited Company with cent percent government ownership and began working as Sonali Bank Limited from November 15, 2007.

Sonali Bank has so far opened two branches in India with a regional head office situated at Kolkata. It also has a strong remittances department to delight customers with an ultimate banking experience.

### 10.12 Oman International Bank

Oman International Bank was established on January 1, 1984 as the first Sultanate's first entirely-owned Omani Commercial Bank. Over the years, it has become one of the largest banks of Oman with a wide network in a large number of countries. Today, the Oman International Bank has a branch chain comprising of 83 branches in the Sultanate of Oman and around five overseas branches, out of which two are present in India and the rest in Pakistan. The Bank also introduced Oman for the first time with ATMs, phone banking and school banking.

The bank has two branches in the major cities of India, one in Mumbai and other in Cochin. The branch of Oman International Bank in Mumbai serves as the country's head office of the bank.

## 10.13 Some Other Foreign Banks in India

**10.13.1 Abu Dhabi Commercial Bank Ltd.:** Abu Dhabi Commercial Bank (ADCB) is one of the most prominent nationalized banks of the United Arab Emirates (UAE). Three different banks viz. the Khalij Commercial Bank, the Emirates Commercial Bank and the Federal Commercial Bank merged in the month of July 1985, leading to the incorporation of the Abu Dhabi Commercial Bank.

**10.13.2 Antwerp Diamond Bank:** The Antwerp Diamond Bank is a small bank that specializes solely in delivering excellent services to the diamond and the diamond jewellery sector. The bank is ranked the second largest diamond bank worldwide.

**10.13.3 Arab Bangladesh Bank:** Arab Bangladesh Bank Limited is one of the leading private sector banks based in Bangladesh. It was instituted on December 31, 1981 and served as the very first private sector bank of the country. The bank commenced its functions from April 12, 1882.

**10.13.4 Bank of Bahrain and Kuwait BSC:** Bank of Bahrain and Kuwait (BBK) was established in Bahrain in March 1971 and provides a range of efficient and personalized banking facilities. The bank established its first overseas branch in Kuwait in 1978.

**10.13.5 Bank of Ceylon:** Bank of Ceylon, popularly abbreviated as BOC, is a government-owned, major commercial bank in Sri Lanka. It was established in 1939 with its head office located in iconic cylindrical building in the capital Colombo, the commercial capital of the island.

**10.13.6 Bank of Nova Scotia:** The Bank of Nova Scotia, famously known as Scotia Bank, is counted amongst North America's leading financial establishments and also the most international of all the Canadian Banks. It stands at the third position in the list of Canada's largest banks.

**10.13.7 Bank of Tokyo-Mitsubishi UFJ Ltd.:** Japan's largest bank, the Bank of Tokyo-Mitsubishi UFJ, Ltd. was founded on January 1, 2006 as a result of a merger between Bank of Tokyo-Mitsubishi, Ltd. and UFJ Bank Ltd. Separately, the Bank of Tokyo-Mitsubishi was established as Mitsubishi Bank, Ltd.

**10.13.8 Chinatrust Commercial Bank Ltd.:** Chinatrust Commercial Bank Limited (CTCB) is amongst the biggest private banks in Taiwan, managed by the family of Koo Chen-Fu. It was founded in the year 1966, initially by the name of China Securities and Investment Corporation.

**10.13.9 Credit Agricole Corporate and Investment Bank:** Credit Agricole Corporate and Investment Bank (Credit Agricole CIB formerly known as Calyon) is the entity of Credit Agricole's corporate and investment banking and was established in May 2004 by the transfer of assets and services from Credit Lyonnais.

**10.13.10 JP Morgan Chase Bank:** An American multinational banking corporation, JP Morgan Chase Bank has been a major provider of financial services and is one of the largest banks in the world. It is the largest bank in United States by sales, profits, assets and market value.

**10.13.11 PT. Bank International Indonesia Tbk.:** Pt. Bank International Indonesia Tbk (BII) was founded on May 15, 1959. The bank post gaining a foreign exchange bank status in the year 1988 enrolled its shares on the Jakarta Stock Exchange and Indonesia Stock Exchange.

**10.13.12 Societe Generale:** One of the oldest banks of France, Societe Generale is a prime European financial services company having a considerable international existence. Tours Societe Generale in the business district of La Defense, Nanterre, west of Paris, serves as its head office.

**10.13.13 VTB Bank:** VTB Bank, formerly known as Vneshtorg Bank, is amongst the leading banks of Russia and the largest in terms of authorized capital. It is a government-owned international bank with a presence in 13 countries. VTB is the second largest bank in Russia.

# 11

# National Bank for Agriculture and Rural Development (NABARD)

---

National Bank for Agriculture and Rural Development (NABARD) was established by an Act of the Parliament on 12th July 1982. The agriculture credit functions of the Reserve Bank of India (RBI) and refinance functions of the then Agricultural Refinance and Development Corporation (ARDC) were transferred to NABARD on its formation. The paid up capital of NABARD is ₹ 2,000 crore, subscribed by the GoI and RBI at ₹ 550 crore and ₹ 1,450 crore respectively. The management of NABARD is vested with a board of directors comprising the chairman, managing director, representatives of RBI, GoI, State Governments, and directors appointed by the GoI.

The mission of NABARD is to promote sustainable and equitable agriculture and rural prosperity through effective credit support, related services, institution development and other innovative initiatives.

The primary objectives of the organization are to:

1. Facilitate credit flow for agriculture, rural infrastructure and rural development.
2. Promote policies, practices and innovations conducive to rural development.
3. Strengthen rural credit delivery system through institutional development.
4. Supervise rural financial institutions (cooperative banks and regional rural banks).
5. Provide consultancy services.

## 11.1 NABARD's Operations in Brief

NABARD's operations include providing financial

services, working towards promotion and development activities, supervision of cooperative banks and RRBs and credit planning.

**11.1.1 Seasonal Agricultural Operations (SAO):** NABARD provides refinance by way of credit limits for financing seasonal agricultural operations at concessional rate of interest to state cooperative banks (SCBs) and regional rural banks (RRBs). To ensure timely availability of credit to farmers for taking up seasonal agricultural operations, banks follow production-oriented system of lending. The assessment of credit requirement is based on area under different crops and crop wise scales of finance.

Refinance support is extended for various other activities, other than SAO, to:

1. Agriculture, allied and marketing activities.
2. Marketing of crops.
3. Pisciculture.
4. Industrial cooperative societies (other than weavers).
5. Labour contract and forest labour cooperative societies including collection of minor forest produce.
6. Rural artisans including weaver members of functional societies.
7. Procurement of agricultural inputs (fertilisers, seeds, etc.).

**11.1.2 Weavers' Finance:** Refinance is extended to state cooperative banks/DCCBs for financing the working capital requirements of primary weavers cooperative societies, individual weavers, handloom weaver groups and master weavers for their production and marketing activities. NABARD also provides refinance assistance to state cooperative banks for financing the apex/regional weavers cooperatives for procurement and marketing of products of primary weavers cooperatives and for trading in yarn. The state handloom development corporations engaged in procuring and marketing of products from decentralized weavers units outside cooperative fold are also extended refinance through state cooperative banks and commercial banks.

The weavers outside the cooperative fold organised into handloom weavers groups on the lines of joint liability groups are supported through cooperative banks, regional rural banks and commercial banks.

## 11.2 Medium-term Credit

**11.2.1 Medium-term (Conversion) Loan:** On State Governments declaring substantial crop loss on account of natural calamities affecting the farmers' ability to repay their production credit dues to banks, refinance by way of medium term loan is granted to state cooperative banks and regional rural banks to enable them to convert their short term loans of farmers into medium term loans. This facilitates the farmers to become eligible for fresh loans.

**11.2.2 Medium-term (non-schematic) Loans:** Refinance is provided to SCBs and RRBs for financing farmers to acquire productive assets for certain approved agricultural investment purposes. Investment credit leads to capital formation through asset creation. It induces technological upgradation resulting in increased production, productivity and incremental income to farmers and entrepreneurs.

## 11.3 Eligible Institutions

NABARD provides refinance support to SCARDBs, SCBs, RRBs, CBs, scheduled primary urban cooperative banks, North East Development Finance Corporation Ltd. (NEDFi), non-banking financial companies (NBFCs), etc. in respect of their term loans extended in the rural areas.

## 11.4 Eligible Purposes for Refinance

Minor and micro irrigation, land development, waste land development, dry land farming, farm mechanisation, plantation and horticulture, animal husbandry, fisheries, storage godowns and market yards, renewable sources of energy, post-harvest management, agro and food processing, hi-tech projects, agri export zones, non-farm sector including rural industries, micro finance, joint liability groups, contract farming, agri-clinic and agri business centres, purchase of land by small/marginal farmers, share croppers, etc., rural housing and disbursements under poverty alleviation programmes like SGSY, SC/ST action plan, etc., are eligible for refinance. NABARD also assists client institutions in techno-economic appraisal of projects in addition to providing refinance.

# 12

# Small Industries Development Bank of India (SIDBI)

SIDBI was established on April 2, 1990. The charter establishing it, The Small Industries Development Bank of India Act, 1989 envisaged SIDBI to be "the principal financial institution for the promotion, financing and development of industry in the small-scale sector and to co-ordinate the functions of the institutions engaged in the promotion and financing or developing industry in the small scale sector and for matters connected therewith or incidental thereto.

The business domain of SIDBI consists of small-scale industrial units, which contribute significantly to the national economy in terms of production, employment and exports. Small-scale industries are the industrial units in which the investment in plant and machinery does not exceed ₹ 1 crore. In addition, SIDBI's assistance flows to the transport, health care and tourism sectors and also to the professional and self-employed persons setting up small-sized professional ventures.

The mission of SIDBI is to empower the micro, small and medium enterprises (MSMEs) sector with a view to contributing to the process of economic growth, employment generation and balanced regional development.

SIDBI has a vision to emerge as a single window for meeting the financial and developmental needs of the MSME sector to make it strong, vibrant and globally competitive, to position SIDBI Brand as the preferred and customer-friendly institution and for enhancement of share holder wealth and highest corporate values through modern technology platform.

## 12.1 Mandatory Objectives

As an apex financial institution for promotion, financing

and development of industry in the small scale sector, SIDBI meets the varied developmental needs of the Indian SSI sector by its wide-ranging promotional and developmental (P&D) activities and this remains its primary objective. The initiatives of the bank is to aim at improving the inherent strength of small-scale sector on one hand as also economic development of poor through promotion of micro-enterprises, development of the small industries, partnership with NGOs, associate financial institutions, corporate bodies, R&D laboratories, marketing agencies, etc..

Development, co-ordination, promotion and financing are the four basic objectives set out in the SIDBI Charter. They have been set out with the goal to attain orderly growth of industry in the small scale sector. The Charter has provided SIDBI considerable flexibility in adopting appropriate operational strategies to meet these objectives. The activities of SIDBI has evolved over the period of time and now meet almost all the requirements of small-scale industries which fall into a wide spectrum constituting modern and technologically superior units at one end and traditional units at the other.

**12.2 Development Outlook**

As envisaged by SIDBI, the major issues which the SSI units are confronting were identified as Technology obsolescence, Managerial inadequacies, incidence of sickness, lack of appropriate infrastructure, lack of marketing network, poor quality and delayed payments. Over the years, SIDBI has put in place financing schemes either through its direct financing mechanism or through indirect assistance mechanism and special focus programmes under its P&D initiatives. In its approach, SIDBI has struck a good balance between financing and providing other support services.

As an apex institution, SIDBI makes use of the network of the banks and state level financial institutions, which have retail outlets. SIDBI supplements the efforts of existing institutions through its direct assistance schemes to reach financial assistance to the ultimate borrowers in the small-scale sector. Refinancing, bills rediscounting, lines of credit and resource support mechanisms have evolved over the period of time to route SIDBI's assistance through the network of other retail institutions in the financial system.

Improved levels of co-ordination for development of the small scale sector is also achieved through a system of dialogue and obtaining feedback from the representatives of institutions of small-scale industries who are on the SIDBI's National Advisory Committee and Regional Advisory Committees.

SIDBI has entered into memoranda of understanding with many banks, governmental agencies, international agencies, research and development institutions and industry associations to facilitate a co-ordinated approach in dealing with the issues for development of small-scale industries. Apart from various banks, some other agencies which have an MoU with SIDBI are as follows:

1. Swiss Agency for Development and Co-operation.
2. Small Industries Development Organisation.
3. Auto Components Manufactures Association.
4. Council for Scientific and Industrial Research.
5. Asia and Pacific Centre for Transfer of Technology.
6. United Nations Industrial Development Organisation.
7. Confederation of Indian Industry.
8. National Research Development Organisation.
9. Government of India for channelising TREAD assistance.
10. Small Enterprise Assistance Funds (SEAF) for setting up of SEAF India SME Equity Fund and for other capacity building initiatives for SMEs.

## 12.3 Promotional Activities

As an apex financial institution for promotion, financing and development of industry in the small-scale sector, SIDBI meets the varied developmental needs of the Indian SSI sector by its wide-ranging promotional and developmental (P&D)

activities. These initiatives aim at improving the inherent strength of small-scale sector on one hand as also economic development of poor through promotion of micro-enterprises. In pursuance of its multifaceted P&D activity, synergistic with its business activities aimed at development of the small industries, SIDBI looks forward to a partnership with NGOs, associate financial institutions, corporate bodies, R&D laboratories, marketing agencies, etc., for national level programmes.

SIDBI has identified the following thrust areas of P&D activities, which are being undertaken in partnership with various institutions, agencies, and NGOs:

To encourage banks to lend more to this sector, Government of India and SIDBI have set up the Credit Guarantee Fund Trust for Micro and Small Enterprises (CGTMSE) in July 2000, to provide credit guarantee support to collateral free/third-party guarantee free loans up to ₹ 100 lakh extended by banks and lending institutions for micro and small enterprise (MSEs) under its Credit Guarantee Scheme (CGS).

**12.3.1 India SME Technology Services Limited:** India SME Technology Services Limited (ISTSL) was set up in November 2005. The purpose was to provide a platform for MSMEs to tap opportunities at the global level for acquisition of modern technologies. ISTSL continues to pursue its strategy of rendering technical services for technology transfer and promotion of energy efficient, environment friendly technologies in the MSME sector. Efforts are being made to facilitate reduction in Green House Gases in the MSME sector.

In order to strengthen and accelerate the process of technological modernization in the MSME sector, ISTSL has entered into partnership with various national and international organizations engaged in similar activities.

SIDBI, along with leading public, foreign and private sector Banks and Dun and Bradstreet Information Services India Private Limited (D&B), set up SME Rating Agency of

India Ltd. (SMERA) in September 2005, as an MSME dedicated third-party rating agency to provide comprehensive, transparent and reliable ratings and risk profiling.

India SME Asset Reconstruction Company Ltd. (ISARC) is the country's first MSME focused Asset Reconstruction Company striving for speedier resolution of non-performing assets (NPA) by unlocking the idle NPAs for productive purposes which would facilitate greater and easier flow of credit from the Banking sector to the MSMEs. Set up in April 2008, ISARC's objective is to acquire NPAs and strive to maximize recovery value through innovative resolution methods. It also complied with the conditions stipulated by RBI while granting the certificate of registration as an ARC and became fully operational from April 15, 2009.

## 12.4 Rural Industries Programme (RIP)

The programme aims at development of viable and self-sustaining tiny/small enterprises in rural and semi urban India by harnessing local entrepreneurial talent. The programme attempts to address the problems such as rural unemployment, urban migration and under-utilisation of local skills and resources, and is designed as a comprehensive business development services programme.

The Rural Industries Programme (RIP) of SIDBI provides a cohesive and integrated package of basic inputs like information, motivation, training and credit, backed by appropriate technology and market linkages for the purpose of enterprise promotion. Long-term viability and sustainability of the enterprises promoted is an important aspect of RIP. New enterprises require continued support, at least for the first year of their operations. Therefore, an amount of ₹ 1,000 per unit is payable to the IAs by way of post-sanction incentive over and above the initial performance fee for providing escort services to the assisted entrepreneurs and post-sanction work. Entrepreneurs are supported for group participation in domestic trade fairs and exhibition-cum-sale for extending marketing support.

The RIP has emerged as a comprehensive programme generating employment for rural poor in industrially backward areas by grounding of enterprises on techno-economic considerations rather than grants/subsidy related considerations. Professional support is provided in identifying ventures, linking them with formal Banking channel after due appraisal, providing escort services at each stage from inception of project with emphasis on technology transfer and long term sustainability. SIDBI's efforts in this direction have been internationally recognised and the RIP has bagged the prestigious "ADFIAP Development Awards 2003" given by the "Association of Development Finance Institutions in Asia and Pacific" (ADFIAP) under the Countryside Development category. The RIP has since been modified to Modified Rural Industries Programme (MRIP) and its salient features are as under.

**12.4.1 Modified Rural Industries Programme (MRIP):** The bank has launched a modified RIP in December 2009, in select underserved areas with focus on setting up of new micro enterprises either with bank linkages or through self-financing. MRIP aims at promoting viable rural enterprises leading to employment generation in rural India by facilitating availability of business services. It would create mechanism to provide help in identifying, motivating and guiding rural entrepreneurs in setting up industrial ventures. It also aims at gainful utilisation of local resources.

### 12.5 Entrepreneurship Development Programme (EDP)

Entrepreneurship can be developed by training. Towards this end and also to make the Entrepreneurship Development Programmes (EDPs) result-oriented, SIDBI has been supporting suitable agencies to train and guide potential entrepreneurs to set up enterprises. EDPs aim at training various target groups in entrepreneurial traits so that they obtain adequate information, motivation and guidance in setting up their own enterprises. In order to maintain a homogeneous nature of participating groups, EDPs focus on rural entrepreneurs, women, SC/ST, minority communities, etc. The EDPs are normally of short duration followed with proper practical training inputs. Training agencies specialized in conducting EDPs, non-governmental organisations (NGOs) and technical institutes are extended assistance to conduct product/process specific EDPs.

## 12.6 Technology Upgradation Programmes

The competitiveness of the products of SSI units both in the domestic and international markets is dependent to a large extent on their productivity levels, price factors and quality characteristics. SIDBI's technology upgradation and modernization programme is aimed at improving the technical capabilities and competitiveness of SSI units in clusters by introducing commercial proven technologies which will result in significant improvement in quality, productivity, bring about cost reduction, saving of energy and raw materials and reduction in the level of pollution. SIDBI's efforts broadly aim at:

1. Creation of awareness on new product/process technologies.
2. Skill upgradation.
3. Development of technology related common facilities for the cluster.
4. Provision of unit-specific modernization package.
5. Energy conservation and introduction of environment friendly technologies.
6. Quality upgradation in terms of systems and products.

The first step involves the selection of clusters, which have certain homogeneity in terms of status of technology, products, production levels, trade practices, and capacity to absorb improved technology. Individual clusters are then assigned to expert consultancy agencies that assess the technology upgradation needs and prepare unit-specific modernisation packages including scope for consolidation of technical capabilities of existing units.

# 13

# Export-Import Bank of India (EXIM Bank)

---

## 13.1 Establishment of EXIM Bank

Exim Bank was set up by an Act of Parliament in September, 1981. It is a wholly-owned subsidiary of Government of India. The EXIM Bank commenced its operations in March, 1982. The main objectives was to provide financial assistance to exporters and importers, and for functioning as the principal financial institution for coordinating the working of institutions engaged in financing export and import of goods and services with a view to promote the country's international trade...". The objective was also to act on business principles with due regard to public interest. Exim Bank of India has evolved into an institution that plays a major role in partnering Indian industries, particularly the small and medium enterprises, in their globalisation efforts, through a wide range of products and services offered at all stages of the business cycle, starting from import of technology and export product development to export production, export marketing, pre-shipment and post-shipment and overseas investment.

The authorised capital of the EXIM Bank is ₹ 200 crore and paid up capital is ₹ 100 crore, wholly subscribed by the Central Government. The bank can raise additional resources through:

1. Loans/grants from Central Government and Reserve Bank of India.
2. Lines of credit from institutions abroad.
3. Funds raised from Euro Currency markets.
4. Bonds issued in India.

Since inception, Exim Bank has had, at the helm of its affairs, leading banking professionals as chief executive officers. Shri R.C. Shah, a seasoned banker, with vast commercial and international banking experience, was the first chairman and managing director of Exim Bank during January 1982-January 1985. His vision helped the setting up of the institution as a unique organizational model, with a flat, non-hierarchical culture, multi-disciplinary approach to problem solving, access to the latest technology and a climate for innovation. He was succeeded by Shri Kalyan Banerji, who was the chairman and managing director during February 1985-April 1993. Shri Banerji had long years of commercial banking experience, with exposure to international banking.

Ms. Tarjani Vakil took over as the chairperson and managing director of the bank in August 1993 and guided the institution in its endeavours for export capability creation, till October 1996. Ms. Vakil had long years of development banking experience and was associated with Exim Bank since its inception. She was succeeded by Shri Y.B. Desai, who was the managing director of the bank during August 1997-April 2001. Shri Desai had vast commercial banking experience and joined Exim Bank in the initial years of the institution. Shri T.C. Venkat Subramanian took over as chairman and managing director of Exim Bank from May 1, 2001. Shri Subramanian had both commercial banking and development banking experience and was associated with Exim Bank since its inception. Under the stewardship of Shri Subramanian, Exim Bank has crossed significant milestones in business promotion as well as other initiatives as the premier export finance institution of the country. Shri T.C.A. Ranganathan is the current CMD w.e.f. April 8, 2010 and is a former deputy managing director of State Bank of India.

## 13.2 Objectives and Functions

The objectives and functions of the Exim Bank include the following:

1. Grant of loans and advances in India solely or jointly with commercial banks to persons exporting or intending to

export Indian goods which may include the export of turnkey projects and civil consultancy services.

2. Grant of lines of credit to Governments, financial institutions and other suitable organizations in foreign countries to enable persons outside India to import from India, goods including turnkey projects, civil construction contracts and other services including consultancy services.
3. Handling transactions where a mix of government credit and commercial credit for exports is involved.
4. Purchasing, discounting and negotiating export bills.
5. Selling or discounting export bills in international markets.
6. Discounting of export bills negotiated or purchased by a scheduled bank or financial institution notified by government, or granting loans and advances against such bills.
7. Providing refinance facilities to specified financial institutions against credits extended by them for specified exports or imports.
8. Granting loans and advances or issuing guarantees solely or jointly with a commercial Bank for the import of goods and services from abroad.
9. Issuing confirmation/endorsing letters of credit on behalf of exporters in India, negotiating, collecting bills under letters of credit, opening letters of credit on behalf of importers of goods and services and negotiating documents received there under.
10. Buying and selling foreign exchange and performing such other functions of an authorized dealer as may be necessary for the functions of an export-import bank.
11. Undertaking and financing research, surveys and techno-economic studies bearing on the promotion and development of international trade.
12. Providing technical, administrative and financial assistance to any exporter in India or any other person who intends to export goods from India for the promotion,

management or expansion of any industry with a view to developing international trade.

The Exim Bank extends both funded and non-funded assistance for promotion of foreign trade. The funded assistance program of the bank includes direct financial assistance to exporters, rediscounting of export bills, technology and consultancy services financing, refinancing of export credit and re-lending facility to banks abroad.

The non-funded assistance is in the form of guarantees which are in the form of bid bonds, advance payment and performance guarantees, retention money guarantees and guarantees for raising finance abroad.

The Exim Bank participates with commercial banks in India in the issuance of guarantees in foreign currencies on behalf of Indian exporters/contractors in favour of overseas importers/employers and banks.

Exim syndication facility was later introduced to attract greater participation in export credit by commercial banks in India who are authorized dealers in foreign exchange. Under this scheme, the Exim Bank provides funds for an export proposal and syndicates the credit risks to commercial banks, and the banks for assuming the risks earn a commission of 0.5 percent per annum from the Exim Bank. The Exim Bank also provides information and advisory services to enable exporters to evaluate the international risks, export opportunities and competitiveness. These include country studies, merchant banking services, advice on international marketing and data to enable effective participation in opportunities offered by projects by multilateral institutions. Further, the bank carries out research and analysis on specific industry sub-sectors with export potential international trade related subjects. These are widely disseminated amongst exporters, academicians, industry and trade organizations and government.

Thus, the Exim Bank follows a three pronged strategy to promote Indian exports. More than export finance, the bank is engaged in export capability creation.

### 13.3 Initiatives by EXIM Bank

1. Exim Bank of India has been the prime mover in encouraging project exports from India. The bank provides Indian project exporters with a comprehensive range of services to enhance the prospect of their securing export contracts, particularly those funded by multilateral funding agencies like the World Bank, Asian Development Bank, African Development Bank and European Bank for Reconstruction and Development.
2. The bank extends lines of credit to overseas financial institutions, foreign governments and their agencies, enabling them to finance imports of goods and services from India on deferred credit terms. Exim Bank's lines of credit obviate credit risks for Indian exporters and are of particular relevance to SME exporters.
3. The bank's Overseas Investment Finance programme offers a variety of facilities for Indian investments and acquisitions overseas. The facilities include loan to Indian companies for equity participation in overseas ventures, direct equity participation by Exim Bank in the overseas venture and non-funded facilities such as letters of credit and guarantees to facilitate local borrowings by the overseas venture.
4. The bank provides financial assistance by way of term loans in Indian rupees/foreign currencies for setting up new production facility, expansion, modernization, and upgradation of existing facilities and for acquisition of production equipment/technology. Such facilities particularly help export oriented small and medium enterprises for creation of export capabilities and enhancement of international competitiveness.
5. Under its export marketing finance programme, Exim Bank supports small and medium enterprises in their export marketing efforts including financing the soft expenditure relating to implementation of strategic and systematic export market development plans.

6. The bank has launched the rural initiatives programme with the objective of linking Indian rural industry to the global market. The programme is intended to benefit rural poor through creation of export capability in rural enterprises.
7. In order to assist the small and medium enterprises, the bank has put in place the export marketing services (EMS) programme. Through EMS, the bank seeks to establish, on best efforts basis, SME sector products in overseas markets, starting from identification of prospective business partners to facilitating placement of final orders. The service is provided on success fee basis.
8. Exim Bank supplements its financing programmes with a wide range of value-added information, advisory and support services, which enable exporters to evaluate international risks, exploit export opportunities and improve competitiveness, thereby helping them in their globalisation efforts.

# 14

# Business Correspondents and Business Facilitators (BCs/BFs)

## 14.1 Introduction to BC/BF

In January 2006, the Reserve Bank of India issued a new set of guidelines allowing banks to employ two categories of intermediaries—business correspondents (BCs) and business facilitators (BFs)—to expand their outreach. According to the guidelines, the BCs are permitted to carry out transactions on behalf of the bank as agents and the BFs can refer clients, pursue the clients' proposal and facilitate the bank to carry out its transactions, but cannot transact on behalf of the bank.

The new guidelines have arrived when a vast array of new technology is available, offering new and inexpensive ways for managing transactions from remotely located offices. The combination of these technological advances with the new guidelines has inspired a number of efforts in India to experiment with the BC/BF model.

These efforts use a variety of new models–for example, POS devices and mobile phones– to secure and process transactions. Some of the efforts include responding to government policy to open 'no frills accounts' and to process Government payments (Government to person-G2P) such as the National Rural Employment Guarantee Scheme, pensions and other social payments.

While all this holds potential for banks, the experiences are mixed and there is a general consensus that the scheme has not taken off in the way it was envisioned. There is a perception that the existing regulations do not allow sufficient flexibility for the BC arrangement to be viable. The experiments underway offer an opportunity to examine the different experiences, different models, choices of technology and the viability. There is also a feeling that most banks have not really given the BC arrangement the kind of push it requires considering its future potential.

**14.2 Financial Inclusion**

Working on a job site under the Mahatma Gandhi National Rural Employment Guarantee Scheme (MGNREGS), Sakuna Bai is eagerly awaiting her next work payment to reach her State Bank of India account. "I have to deposit my daughter's school fees," says the 30-year-old mother of three from Agrakhurd village, in Bagli Block of Dewas district in Madhya Pradesh. The bank account has been opened under NREGS and since 2008, when wages started getting directly transferred to workers' bank accounts. Sakuna Bai has understood the importance of savings. "When we were paid in cash, there was hardly any money to spare".

Borrowing money from moneylenders was always risky," she says. But for the past three years, life has become a little better for the family of seven, with both Sakuna and her husband getting work under NREGS. "I was initially hesitant to go to a bank. I had no idea about the working procedure," she adds. Now she operates her husband's account too. "My husband has never set foot in the bank, except once while the account was being created. It's me who operates both accounts," says a proud Sakuna Bai. Sakuna is just one face of the world's 'biggest financial inclusion programme', which NREGS has unintentionally become, with over 10 crore saving accounts opened in both banks and post offices. Crores like Sakuna Bai are still awaiting to access the financial services. Financial inclusion is that tool which will facilitate the same. Financial inclusion is the availability of banking services at an affordable cost to disadvantaged and low-income groups.

A starting point was made through the Khan Committee recommendations as early as 2005 as a prelude to the later day recommendations of the Rangarajan Committee in early 2008. Financial inclusion may be defined as the process of ensuring access to financial services and timely and adequate credit where needed by vulnerable groups such as weaker sections and low income groups at an affordable cost. Financial inclusion is a process of (bringing) the poor, weaker sections and vulnerable groups, (for whom) access to financial services, including credit, timely (on time, when they require the most) at an affordable cost or a price one feels possible to absorb service rendered. The task of financial inclusion as a goal and target aimed was gigantic.

## 14.3 Some Successful Models of Financial Inclusion

**14.3.1 Financial Inclusion in Brazil:** *Branchless banking*: Access to banking through agents called banking correspondents (BCs).

*The Context*: Even though BCs had existed in Brazil since the 1970s, the real boost came a little more than a decade ago when the regulation broadened the range of services that can be offered by BCs and eased several other restrictions. The new laws came in the context of very low penetration of banking services in that country. In 1997, as many as 4 crore Brazilians out of the total 6.2 crore did not have access to any financial services.

*The Experience*: Over the last decade, the model has grown rapidly. Brazil's 150,000 BCs account for about 62 percent of the total number of points of service in the financial system. It is the world's largest such network. Meanwhile, the total number of bank accounts in Brazil has doubled between 2000 and 2008, from 6.37 crore to 12.57 crore.

*The Relevance*: India had tried out pygmy deposit agents in the 1970s but the experience was not good. These agents went about claiming to be bank employees and that led to a lot of disputes and litigation. In fact, RBI Deputy Governor Usha Thorat says, "Brazil, too, has the same problem".

Now that India is ushering in a BC system, the lessons from Brazil are important. The one reason why the system worked there is that the authorities established a strong business case for BCs. For example, the payment of bills of any kind is required to be done through the banking system using a standard form called Boletos. Bill payments comprise 75 percent of volume (1.6 billion) and 70 percent of value (US$ 105 billion) transacted through Brazilian correspondents in 2008.

But in India, there is a very large informal system for transactions that authorities have failed to bring into the Banking system so far. Because unlike Brazil, India has not yet demonstrated a business case for the banks or even the agents," says Greg Chen of CGAP.

**14.3.2 South Africa:** No-frills banking: Basic bank accounts with negligible minimum deposit and a set number of free transactions.

South Africa is one of the most expensive banking markets and the poor cannot afford it. The central bank asked a collective of five banks to launch a 'no-frill' bank account scheme. Launched in 2004, the Mzansi account has no monthly fees. Five transactions in a month are free.

According to a 2009 report by the non-profit Fin Mark Trust, there are 60 lakh Mzansi accounts in a country of 3.2 crore. Some sections of the informal economy, such as employers paying salaries in cash, have come into the banking system thanks to Mzansi.

But all is not rosy. Only 35 lakh out of the 60 lakh accounts are active. That is a usage rate of only 58 percent. "Such accounts have been largely marketed as a pure savings product but what drives usage is transaction—transfer of money, payment of bills etc.," says Ignacio Mas, deputy director, financial services for the poor discipline at the Bill and Melinda Gates Foundation.

The banks have kept further transactions quite expensive. "Once you exhaust the first five transactions which are free, the Mzansi is one of the most expensive accounts in the world," says Jennifer Isern, South Asia head of the access to finance division of IFC.

India has an even more dismal record with its no-frill account plan. The percentage of active accounts is very low although banks have been able to open a large number of accounts. The scheme will begin to work better when more friendly avenues of banking such as kiosks and mobile phones reach a large number of people. Also, the country should encourage a transaction-led model.

**14.3.3 Kenya:** *Bank without a bank*: Do away with the need to have a bank account. Use the mobile phone company as a conduit for keeping and transacting money.

*The Context*: In Kenya, for every bank account, there are two mobile phone connections. And mobile phone use is growing faster than bank account penetration. So, Kenyan authorities ushered in a system where a mobile phone company could act as the repository of customers' money and allow them to transact. However, it can't use that money and the customers don't get any interest.

Safaricom-Vodafone launched M-PESA in 2007 creating this parallel banking ecosystem. The transactions, capped at US$ 500, happen in real time through a wide network of around 17,000 "agents."

*The Experience*: M-PESA has grown rapidly to have an estimated client base of around 1 crore, roughly 40 percent of Kenya's adult population. In fact, when the controversial Kenyan Presidential elections of 2007-08 led to widespread protests and the shutdown of formal banking channels, it was M-PESA that most of the country turned to. Since May 2010, Safaricom has ventured into providing deposit facility too by tying up with Equity Bank. The "M-KESHO" savings account, as it is called, too can be accessed from a customer's mobile phone.

*The Relevance*: In India, the RBI does not allow mobile phone companies to operate as banking channels. In fact, Safaricom's virtual monopoly in the business in Kenya makes many independent observers nervous. "Limiting the number of players who are trying to provide financial inclusion seems a bit counter-productive. For a transformative change, we need as much competition as possible," says Mas.

But there is no reason why India should not allow an M-PESA-like model with plenty of competition. "It will happen if you let some of the creative and entrepreneurial powers in the country to experiment a little bit," says Chen.

**14.3.4 Mexico:** *A Super-efficient lending mission*: Focus on micro credit and allied products. Build enormous scale with supreme efficiency and the power of private capital.

*The Context*: It was Banco Compartamos—which had begun as a non-profit organisation—that showed that microfinance is a business of scale and that private capital can help achieve that scale. It believes an MFI can succeed only by being extremely profitable for its shareholders. Today, a large number of MFIs, especially in India, are embracing the model.

*The Experience*: With 15 lakh clients, Compartamos is the largest MFI in Latin America. The company's interest rates are above 100 percent a year, much worse than the 30 percent levels seen in India. So, its US$ 400-million IPO in 2007 proved controversial. However, nobody disputes Compartamos is where it is today due to the combination of efficiency, innovation and a tight leash on costs. "It is an organisation which has been very efficient at training and managing a very de-centralised base of loan officers. It is fundamentally an HR machine," says Mas.

*The Relevance*: The profit-led model is here to stay. However, Compartamos' success with investors has to do a lot with its 100 percent-plus interest rate. The company charges such rates because loan sharks there charge even more and there is little competition. In India, there are over 1,000 MFIs. Such pricing power will neither be available in India nor tolerated. The long-term success of MFIs rests on being seen as socially helpful.

### 14.4 BC/BF Banking Channel

Banks operate a number of channels through which they

deliver financial services: branches, ATMs and the internet are the traditional channels. The guidelines are written in a way which requires a bank to be involved and is the ultimate provider of services. While RBI has oversight and regulatory responsibility for the BC banking channel as part of its regulatory regime, the principal Banks are responsible for the acts of their correspondents.

This new channel works through a process of collaboration by the bank with one or more partners. These partners often include:

Technology vendors, who provide a range of hardware and processing capacity and connectivity can link clients to BCs and BCs to the bank.

Business correspondents/facilitators are organizations or individuals that organize and offer one or more points of transaction outside of bank branches. The BCs organize and manage a network of such transaction points in partnership with a bank. The business correspondent option offers a new channel through which banks can extend services. The purposes for engaging BC/BF are:

1. To ensure greater financial inclusion and increase outreach of banks in the rural and semi-urban areas.
2. To provide comprehensive financial services to the underprivileged encompassing savings, credit, remittance, insurance, Mutual funds and pension products in a cost effective manner, particularly in untapped/unbanked areas.
3. To improve process efficiencies and reduce transaction costs by providing linkages between the existing network of bank branches and the informal and formal agencies engaged with the poor, by adopting technology based solutions.
4. To leverage on the strengths of intermediaries in accelerating the process of financial inclusion.

Customer service points, are individuals, shops or other outlet points which are responsible for the direct contact with the clients. CSPs open bank accounts, conduct KYC, cash out withdrawals, receive payments and in some cases, extend credit.

**14.5 Guidelines for Business Correspondents (BC)**

The scheduled commercial banks including regional rural banks (RRBs) and local area banks (LABs) may engage business correspondents (BCs) subject to formulation of a policy for engaging business correspondents (BCs) with the approval of their board of directors.

Due diligence may be carried out on the individuals/entities to be engaged as BCs prior to their engagement.

The due diligence exercise may, inter alia, cover aspects such as: (i) reputation/market standing, (ii) financial soundness, (iii) management and corporate governance, (iv) cash handling ability, and (v) ability to implement technology solutions in rendering financial services.

The banks may engage the following individuals/entities as BC.

1. Individuals like retired bank employees, retired teachers, retired government employees and ex-servicemen, individual owners of kirana/medical/fair price shops, individual public call office (PCO) operators, agents of small savings schemes of Government of India/insurance companies, individuals who own petrol pumps, authorized functionaries of well-run self-help groups (SHGs) which are linked to banks, any other individual including those operating common service centres (CSCs).
2. NGOs/ MFIs set up under societies/trust Acts and Section 25 Companies.
3. Cooperative societies registered under mutually aided cooperative societies Acts/cooperative societies Acts of States/Multi State Cooperative Societies Act.
4. Post offices.
5. Companies registered under the Indian Companies Act,

1956 with large and widespread retail outlets, excluding non-banking financial companies (NBFCs).

**14.5.1 Scope of Activities:** The scope of activities may include: (i) identification of borrowers, (ii) collection and preliminary processing of loan applications including verification of primary information/data, (iii) creating awareness about savings and other products and education and advice on managing money and debt counselling, (iv) processing and submission of applications to banks, (v) promoting, nurturing and monitoring of self-help groups/joint liability groups/credit groups/others, (vi) post-sanction monitoring, (vii) follow-up for recovery, (viii) disbursal of small value credit, (ix) recovery of principal/collection of interest, (x) collection of small value deposits, (xi) sale of micro insurance/mutual fund products/ pension products/other third party products, and (xii) receipt and delivery of small value remittances/other payment instruments.

The activities to be undertaken by the BCs would be within the normal course of the bank's banking business, but conducted through the BCs at places other than the bank premises/ATMs.

The banks may use the services of the BC for preliminary work relating to account opening formalities. However, ensuring compliance with KYC and AML norms under the BC model continues to be the responsibility of banks. The banks have to ensure the preservation and protection of the security and confidentiality of customer information in the custody or possession of BC. The banks are required to ensure that equipment and technology used by the BC are of high standards.

## 14.6 Guidelines for Business Facilitators (BF)

**14.6.1 Business Facilitator Model:** The banks may engage the following individuals/entities as BF.

1. NGOs.
2. SHGs.

3. Farmer's Clubs.
4. Functional cooperatives.
5. Community based organizations.
6. IT-enabled rural outlets of corporate entities.
7. Well-functioning Panchayats.
8. Rural multipurpose kiosks/village knowledge centres.
9. Agri clinics/agri business centres.
10. Krishi Vigyan Kendras.
11. KVIC/KVIB units.
12. Post offices.
13. Insurance agents.
14. Social organizations.
15. Individuals such as retired post masters and retired school/college teachers.
16. Individuals such as auto dealers and FMCG stockists, postal agents, insurance agents of private insurance companies (IRDA certified).
17. Retired government employees, ex-servicemen and retired bank employees.
18. Common services centres (CSCs) established by service centre agencies (SCAs) under the National e-Governance Plan (NeGP).

**14.6.2 Scope of Activities:** The scope of activities may include: (i) conduct only non-financial business activities i.e., no cash transactions/handling, (ii) identification of potential customers and activities, (iii) collection and preliminary processing of loan applications/account opening forms for deposits including verification of primary information/data, (iv) filling of loan applications/account opening forms including nomination clause and submission to the bank, (v) cross-selling of other financial products like insurance/mutual fund products/pension products/any other third party product, (vi) assisting in post-sanction monitoring and follow-up for recovery (only after complying with RBI instructions on recovery agents) (vii) promoting and nurturing self-hHelp groups (SHGs)/joint liability groups

(JLGs), wherever relevant, (viii) creating awareness about savings and other products and education and advice on managing money and debt counselling (ix) term deposits of minimum 6 months tenure will be sourced by BF, and (x) as the entire objective of permitting bank to use business facilitator/correspondent model is to extend savings and loan facilities to the under privileged and unbanked population, these models should not be utilized for collecting NRE/NR(O)/FCNR(B) deposits which are generally of a large value.

**14.7 Consumer Protection Measures**

The banks are to take measures to protect the interests of the customers. Some safeguards are outlined below:

1. The retail outlet/sub-agent of the BC should be personally introduced to the members of public by the bank officials in the presence of village elders and government functionaries in a public meeting so that there is no misrepresentation/impersonation.
2. The products and processes should be approved by the banks and the company should not introduce any product/process without the approval of the bank concerned.
3. Each retail outlet/sub-agent may be required to post a signage indicating their status as service providers for the bank as also disclose the name of the BC, the telephone number of the base branch/controlling office of the bank and the banking ombudsman and the fees for all services available at the outlet.
4. Financial services offered by the retail outlets/sub-agents of the BC should not be tied to the sale of any product of such company.
5. The charges for offering various services should be indicated in a brochure and made available at the retail outlets/with the sub-agents.
6. The banks should develop suitable training modules in the

local language(s) in order to provide proper attitudinal orientation and skills to the BCs/sub-agents.

7. As a measure of social audit, there could be periodic block level meetings where members of public are invited along with the BCs operating in the area as also the linked branch managers to express their difficulties and to obtain feedback. Lead district manager (LDM) of the lead bank could attend such meetings in the district to get a direct feedback and provide such feedback to the controlling offices.
8. The bank should have necessary business continuity plan (BCP) in place to ensure uninterrupted service in case the agency arrangement with the companies/sub-agents is terminated.
9. In case a company is engaged as BC by more than one Bank, it should be ensured that the customer database and account details are kept separate and there is no co-mingling of data.

### 14.8 Advantages of Using BC/BFs

1. **Better Alternative Than Bank Branches:** Normally, a rural bank branch can serve 3,000 to 4,000 families in 12 to 15 villages within a radius of 15 kms. A public sector bank branch may require more than 5 years to breakeven in unbanked areas in India, while a private sector and foreign bank with IT connectivity may require about 5 times more. The BC option potentially enables banks to reach out much faster and at a much lower cost.
2. **Reaching the Unreached:** The model enables banks to extend financial services to the unreached clients beyond their branch network as beneficiaries of the BCs are mostly located at un-banked and under-banked areas.
3. **Doorstep Banking:** Disbursement and loan recovery at the doorsteps of the beneficiary.
4. **Better Quality of Assets:** Target clients are well known to local NGOs, post offices, BDOs and similar local social

bodies, thus loan facilitation by the NGOs/BCs (who are the promoter/builder of the groups) enhances quality of assets.

**14.9 Viability issues for BC/BFs**

1. **Inactive 'No Frills Accounts':** The majority of no frill accounts opened by BCs are not operational. In some locations that have achieved 100 percent financial inclusion, the accounts in use have been less than 25 percent. The average balances in savings accounts have been very low at unviable levels for banks.
2. **Model Viability:** There's a shortage of funding to BCs for meeting the group promotion costs in the case of SHG-bank linkage models. In addition, there are financial constraints on the part of the BCs for capacity-building initiatives, such as investing in training for their staff.
3. **BCs Losing Money:** Initial losses are forcing many BCs to shut their operations. Business continuity risk in such cases is impacting banks adversely. It is time-consuming, costly and ineffective for banks to substitute these BCs with new entrants.

Financial literacy and customer education should form an important part of the business strategy and should form part of the commitment by banks adopting the BC model. Banks may scale up their efforts substantially towards educating their clientele in their respective vernacular languages regarding the benefits of banking habit.

# 15

# Alternate Banking Channels

## 15.1 Introduction

On June 27, 1967 the first "cash machine" colloquially called as "hole on the walls" and was described as "mini-banks" which was designed to allow customers access to cash 24 hours a day. This is the origin of the alternate delivery channel for banks services.

On the 40th Birthday of the "cash machines" John Shepherd Barron, the inventor of the ATM, said: "I am delighted that the cash machine is still going strong. I remember back in 1965 that I would always take money out of my bank on a Saturday morning. However, one Saturday I was one minute late at my bank and it was closed. I had to ask my local garage to cash my cheque. That night I started thinking that there must be a better way to get cash when I wanted it. I thought of the chocolate vending machine where money was put in a lot and a bar dispatched—surely money could be dispensed in the same way. Within two years my idea had become reality and we opened the first cash machine at Barclays Enfield."

John Warren, head of ATMs for Barclays Bank, said: "The hole in the wall or cash machine, more than any other banking innovation, has had a major impact on the way we all conduct our lives, not just our banking. Forty years ago, cash was only available from 9-3 pm; Monday to Friday and Saturdays from 9 -12.30 pm, and as cash was king, queues outside branches on a Saturday morning to get weekend money were common. Now you can get money anytime, anywhere".

Branchless banking is a distribution channel strategy used for delivering financial services without relying on bank branches. While the strategy may complement an existing bank branch network for giving customers a broader range of channels through which they can access financial services, branchless banking can also be used as a separate channel strategy that entirely foregoes bank branches.

By the definition, branchless banking comprises essentially all of the following elements:

1. Use of technology, such as payment cards or mobile phones, to identify customers and record transactions electronically and, in some cases, to allow customers to initiate transactions remotely.
2. Use of (exclusive or nonexclusive) third-party outlets, such as post offices and small retailers, that act as agents for financial services providers and that enable customers to perform functions that require their physical presence, such as cash handling and customer due diligence for account opening.
3. Offer of at least basic cash deposit and withdrawal in addition to transactional or payment services.
4. Backing of a government-recognized, deposit-taking institution, such as a formally licensed bank.
5. Structuring of the above so that customers can use these banking services on a regular basis (available during normal business hours) and without needing to go to bank branches at all, if that's what they choose.

Over the past few years, we have seen core banking system rollouts happening in thousands of branches across the country–with banks grappling with the challenges of implementation and rollout. The fundamentals of banking may remain the same, but the manner in which we perceive 'value', from banking services has been changing almost every six months. This is due to the pace at which technology is changing and the means and tools that technology provides us with. Today, if a bank can assure its customer of a viable 24x7 interface, it has a hope of retaining the customer for longer time. Today, information technology (IT) not only facilitates automation of process and data processing but also provides more value addition to the entire banking business.

As technology ingrains itself in all aspects of a bank's functioning, the challenge lies in exploiting the potential for profiting from investments made in technology. A lot needs to be done on the technological front to keep in pace with the global economies. Alternate delivery channels (ADC) are considered a solution that will bring in efficiencies, bring scale and increase outreach at a relatively lower operational costs. Technology plays a major role in the development of alternate channels and interactions between customers and banks.

Banking industry is experiencing rapid changes due to availability and usage of alternate channels. The market offers a large number of new technologies that allows customers to satisfy many needs at their convenience and with minimum human intervention. With the availability of technology channels, Banks recognise that customers have wider options in terms of accessing Banking services wherever and whenever they desire. Banks in India have started using technology in a proactive manner. The huge number of bank customers and their myriad needs are being met in increasingly sophisticated ways. In a number of areas, the foreign banks and the new private sector banks have been the first movers in the application of technology, but public sector banks are also catching up.

One major advantage that Indian banks have is the availability of major IT companies in India who are the world leaders in IT applications. In addition to significant cost reduction, alternative delivery channels expand outreach to areas in which the traditional bricks and mortar approach is unfeasible, and also increases product diversification by making savings and remittance products convenient, efficient and profitable. Alternate banking delivery channels are new channels and methods for providing banking services directly to customers. We can include internet banking channel, e-banking, intelligent electronic device, ATM, kiosk, or touch tone telephone credit cards, debit cards, net banking, home banking and mobile banking. In fact, mobile banking has successfully accelerated financial inclusion and changed the financial landscape in many developing countries. Mobile phones are compensating for inadequate infrastructure, slow postal services, and the limited coverage of banking systems.

## 15.2 Challenges Ahead

Continuous innovation on the product offerings by banks is paramount to ensure that their products stand out from the crowd. A lot of effort and innovation from banks is required to make their product the preferred choice of the customer. This needs to be backed by a powerful and customized loyalty program for customers to be continuously encouraged to keep using their card. Service is an extremely vital cog in the wheel and the Banks which make the investment to have superior service levels as their USP will have a clear advantage.

Investment in providing a chat interface as a service channel for routine enquiries would be in line with times to come. Ten years ago, a customer would have been happy to Bank with those who provided just a fixed deposit or a recurring deposit in addition to his savings account and a credit card. Today, there is a need to spread the wealth around, diversify the savings into shares, fixed deposits, mutual funds, pension products and insurance. Banks have a choice–offer all these as part of their convenience banking to customers or lose him. This desire and the compulsion to be the one-stop shop for the entire customer's investment and borrowing needs will ensure a lot of banks adopt this model increasingly.

Smart cards embedded with microprocessors or memory chips will become tamper proof and replace the existing plastic cards, offering customers a secure digital identity. This will also provide convenience to customers; provide access to bank's website and individual accounts, accurate tracking of usage, spend analysis and manage long term customer relationships through efficient, timely and valuable services to them.

Biometric ATMs will replace the conventional ATMs across the country, apart from all banks investing in additional ATMs. Banks can authenticate the identity of the customer in three ways; most common being something the user knows (passwords or personal identification numbers), something the user has (a security token etc.) or something the user is (a physical characteristic like fingerprint, palm geometry etc., called as biometric). With increasing threats on compromise of passwords and account takeovers and misuse of cards, biometric form of authentication (which have withstood the test of scrutiny coming out as the most secure form) for ATM and POS transactions would be the way ahead. Statistics show that India's ATM density is around 35 ATMs per 10 lakh people which is abysmally low compared to the US's ATM density of 1300. This is an area of focus for many banks clearly, offering a branding and marketing proposition for their investments apart from interchange revenues on usage.

Cheques will gradually be phased out and replaced by RTGS and NEFT and other electronic forms of money transfers and payment mechanisms offering superior turnaround times. Operational efficiency in processing electronic payment mechanisms will undergo a radical change, with the beneficiary receiving the credit real time online.

Given their dependence on technology for conducting their day-to-day operations, Banks are up against huge challenges such as technology obsolescence, dependence on vendors due to outsourcing of IT services, vendor-related concentration risk, and external threats leading to cyber frauds/crime.

Further, banks face challenges in the form of higher impact due to intentional or unintentional acts of internal employees, new social engineering techniques employed to acquire customers' confidential credentials, need for governance processes to adequately manage technology and information security, need for appreciation of cyber laws and their impact, and to ensure continuity of business processes in the event of major exigencies.

Technology risks not only have a direct impact–operational risks–on a bank but can also exacerbate other risks such as credit risks and market risks. Inadequate technology implementation can also induce strategic risk as decision-making could be based on inaccurate data/information. Compliance risk is also an outcome in the event of non-adherence to any regulatory or legal requirements arising out of the use of IT. These issues, according to the report, ultimately have the potential to impact the safety and soundness of a Bank and in extreme cases may lead to systemic crisis.

In view of the new age challenges being faced by banks on information security, electronic Banking, technology risk management and cyber frauds, the working group exhaustively covered various areas such as IT governance, information security, electronic banking channels such as internet, mobile, ATMs, IT operations, IT services outsourcing, information system audit, cyber frauds, business continuity planning, customer education and legal issues.

The Indian Banks' Association along with the Institute for Development and Research in Banking Technology have been tasked with the responsibility of putting in place industry-wide measures to translate the recommendations of the working group into concrete action so as to realise tangible benefits for the banking industry. The central bank wants actionable and time bound measures on the relevant recommendations in consultation with other stakeholders.

# 16

# Cyber Crimes and the Banking Sector

## 16.1 Introduction

Today, technology is central to the design and delivery of banking services. The modern-day banking services are critically dependent on technological innovation and improvement. Electronic crime started during the period of 1960s in the form of "hacking". In the period of 1970s, presence of computer introduced new crimes as computer crimes in the form of privacy violation, phone tapping, trespassing and distribution of illicit material. Then, later in the period of 1980s electronic systems crime emerged in the form of software piracy, copyright violations and introduction of viruses. The extent of damage after 1980s increased due to the highly sophisticated electronic systems. These electronic crimes had a wider impact on the Indian market, international market, banking sector and other areas also.

In the present globalized scenario, information technology is the most important and controversial term. It is the most powerful technology which is fast, quick and accurate in all sectors. Increased use of information and communication technology (ICT) such as computers, mobile phones, Internet, and other associated technologies are the routes which gave emergence to lot of constructive work as well as destructive work. The destructive activities are considered as "electronic crime" which includes spamming, credit card fraud, ATM frauds, Money laundering, phishing, identity theft, denial of service, etc. Computers and internet are also the new powerful information tools in the present era and these new technologies bring out new threats such as denial of service attacks, viruses, unauthorized entry, information tampering, cyber stalking, spamming and much more.

Cyber crime is emerging as a serious threat. World-wide, governments, police departments and intelligence units have started to react. Initiatives to curb cross border cyber threats are taking shape. The world of Internet today has become a parallel form of life and living. Public are now capable of doing things which were not imaginable few years ago. Internet is fast becoming a way of life for millions of people and also away of living because of growing dependence and reliance of mankind on these machines. Internet has enabled the use of website communication, email and a lot of anytime anywhere IT solutions for the betterment of human kind.

Internet, though offering great benefits to society, also presents opportunities for crime using new and highly sophisticated technology tools. Today e-mail and websites have become the preferred means of communication. Organizations provide Internet access to their staff. By their very nature, they facilitate almost instant exchange and dissemination of data, images and variety of material. This includes not only educational and informative material but also information that might be undesirable or anti-social.

With the advent of computers (and especially the Internet) businesses are subject to threats of malicious activities and cyber-crimes. Cyber criminals use computers and technology to carry out the destructive activities that have been around for decades. Whether it is insiders or unknown intruders involved in hacking (i.e. the unauthorized use or attempt to circumvent the security mechanisms of an information system or network), cracking (i.e. breaking into a computer system), phishing (i.e. attempting to acquire identifiers and passwords), or phreaking (i.e. cracking a phone or communication network), as long as people are the weakest link, there really is no safe harbour from cyber crime.

Information technology has become the backbone of the banking system. It provides a tremendous support to the ever increasing challenges and banking requirements. Presently, banks cannot think of introducing financial product without the presence of information technology. A computer can be the target of an offence when unauthorized access of computer network occurs and on the other hand it affects e-commerce. The banking sector consists of public sector, private sector and foreign banks apart from smaller regional and cooperative banks. In the market, various IT-based banking products, services and solutions are available.

The most common of them are: phone banking; ATM facility; credit, debit and smart cards; internet banking and mobile banking; SWIFT network and INFINET network; connectivity of bank branches to facilitate anywhere banking. The banking sector in India is on the verge of revolutionary changes in the way it functions and delivers its services to customers. The traditional "brick-and mortar" bank branches are getting "networked" and becoming an integral part of an enterprise wide banking platform, called "core banking solutions". Cyber-related crimes, therefore, present an especially high risk to certain industries and types of businesses, including banking industry.

The present contemporary epoch has replaced these traditional monetary instruments from a paper and metal based currency to "plastic money" in the form of credit cards, debit cards, etc. This has resulted in the mounting use of ATMs all over the world. The utilization of ATMs is not only safe but also convenient but safety and convenience, unfortunately, has an evil side. This evil side is reflected in the form of "ATM frauds".

Credit card fraud has become ordinary on internet which not only affects card holders but also online merchants. Credit card fraud can be completed by taking over the account, skimming or if the card is stolen. The term "Internet fraud" refers usually to any type of fraud scheme that uses one or more components of the Internet—such as chat rooms, e-mail, message boards, or web sites with fraudulent solicitations to prospective victims, to conduct fraudulent transactions, or to broadcast the proceeds of fraud to financial institutions or to others connected with the scheme

Cyber crime is a term used to broadly describe criminal activity in which computers or computer networks are a tool, a target, or a place of criminal activity and include everything from electronic cracking to denial of service attacks. It is also used to include traditional crimes in which computers or networks are used to enable illicit activity.

## 16.2 Common Cyber Crime Risks of Financial Institutions

The terms computer crime, high-tech crime, digital crime, e-crime and cyber-crime can be used interchangeably with electronic crime. E-crimes are essentially crimes where the computer is used either as a tool to commit the crime, as a storage device, or as a target of the crime. As a storage device, computers can either store information that will assist in the execution of the crime or information that is illegal for the owners to possess, such as stolen intellectual property. Computers are classified as a target if the information that they contain is altered or retrieved in an unlawful way, such crimes can range from amateur hacking to terrorism.

Some common cyber crime risks are as under:

1. Phishing.
2. Identity theft.
3. Worms and trojan horses.
4. Spyware.
5. Search engines/Google.
6. Denial-of-service/distributed-denial of- service attacks.
7. Debit/credit card cloning.
8. Hacking.

**16.2.1 Phishing:** Phishing (pronounced "fishing") is growing rapidly. Phishing relies on the ability of the perpetrators fool (or con) a victim, and that usually involves 'spoofing'. Spoofing is the imitation (or mimicking) of a legitimate website, e-mailer entity communication in order to trick the recipient into believing the communication or website is trustworthy. Thus, phishing involves the use of seemingly legitimate communications (that is, spoofed) to deceive bank customers into disclosing sensitive information, such as bank account information, social security numbers, credit card data, passwords or financial personal identification numbers (PIN). Most often, the purpose of phishing is to gain sufficient information to perpetrate a fraud.

For example, a perpetrator will create a fraudulent e-mail message that looks legitimate and arrives from an apparently trustworthy source. The legitimacy comes from copying the bank's logo or graphics from its website and inserting it into the document, along with official-looking signature files and contact information. The trusted source is not only the spoofed e-mail but a spoofed website as well.

The e-mail, accompanied by a high sense of urgency, usually directs or links the recipient to a purported website of the spoofed bank. In reality, the person is being directed to an illegitimate website where perpetrators will ask for information to serve their criminal intents. Often the spoofed uniform resource locator (URL or web address) will be similar to the real entity's address.

**16.2.2 ID Theft:** One good definition of ID theft for financial institutions is provided by Visa, "ID theft involves manipulating or improperly accessing another person's identifying information, such as PAN number, mother's maiden name, account number, or PIN (rather than account number) in order to fraudulently establish credit or take over a deposit, credit or other financial account for benefit". ID theft is closely associated with phishing. That is, ID theft is often made possible because of a successful phishing scheme, where sufficient information is captured to steal that person's identity and then perpetrate fraud using that person's identity. ID theft, however, has been perpetrated successfully in the past without the use of phishing and still is perpetrated using other methods or means. ID theft is almost always employed as a means to commit other crimes. Banks have generally had sound controls to secure this kind of sensitive and risky data. But that information can be gathered by physical means, such as dumpster dives or social engineering, as well as cyber means, such as phishing, although phishing is clearly becoming more popular. Softer targets, such as bank branches, carry a higher risk of being the target for social engineering or ID theft.

**16.2.3 Worm and Trojan Horse:** A worm is a program (or algorithm) that replicates itself over a computer network and usually performs a malicious action, such as using up the computer's resources and possibly shutting the system down. It is similar to a virus. Unlike worms and viruses, trojan horses do not replicate themselves but they can be just as destructive. One of the most insidious types of trojan horse is a program that claims to rid your computer of viruses but instead introduces viruses onto your computer. Another typical malicious use of a trojan horse is to have it "sit" on a system and capture keyboard strokes and send them back to the perpetrator. This process provides the perpetrator the potential ability to steal passwords and IDs, especially for online banking. A good example of worms and trojan horses that target financial institutions would be the Bugbear family. Bugbear is a mass-mailing worm that spreads through networks.

It also infects a select list of executable files. Bugbear possesses keystroke logging and backdoor capabilities and may even disable the system' anti-virus software. It specifically handles infections at financial institutions differently than other infections. This functionality will cause the worm to send sensitive banking data (files peculiar to banking computer systems and deliberately sought by the worm Bugbear) to one of 10 hard-coded, public internet email addresses. The sent information includes cached passwords and key-logging data. Other trojan horses and key-loggers can be used in the same manner to retrieve user names and passwords for online financial accounts.

**16.2.4 Spyware:** An emerging tactic for cyber criminals and crackers/hackers is spy ware. A spy ware is any software that covertly gathers user information through the user's internet connection without his or her knowledge, usually for advertising purposes. Spyware ranges from harmless pop-up ads to the ability to record anything that happens on a computer and then transmit that data to a remote site. For example, 'Win What Where' software can record all keystrokes on a personal computer and send them to some remote location on the Internet. Spyware applications are typically bundled as a hidden component of freeware or shareware programs that can be downloaded from the Internet.

Once installed, the spyware monitors user activity on the Internet and transmits that information in the background to someone else. Spyware can also gather information about e-mail addresses and even passwords and credit card numbers. Aside from the questions of ethics and privacy, spy ware steals from the user by using the computer's memory resources and also by eating bandwidth as it sends information back to the spy ware's home base via the user's Internet connection. Because spyware is using memory and system resources, the applications running in the background can lead to system crashes or general system instability. They have the ability to monitor keystrokes, scan files on the hard drive, snoop other applications (such as chat programs or word processors), install other spyware programs, read cookies and change the default homepage on the Web browser—consistently relaying this information back to the spyware author who could use it for advertising/marketing purposes, sell the information to another party or use it to perpetrate ID theft. Spyware may sound like viruses or a Trojan horse. It is hard to tell the difference and there is not as strong an anti-spyware awareness, or as many anti-spyware tools, as is the case with antivirus software.

**16.2.5 Search Engines:** One key cyber-tool used by criminals is the Internet search engine, such as Google. For instance, credit card numbers are easily pulled. Bank account numbers can be found if placed improperly on the Web. In addition to sensitive information, sensitive resources can be obtained, such as secure login pages not published to the general public. This misuse of Google is referred to as "Google hacking".

**16.2.6 Denial of Service (DoS):** DoS is intended to harm victims by bringing computer systems to a screeching halt, specifically servers, such as online banking servers that provide Internet access to bank transactions and data. When financial institutions' online banking services are down, not only are business operations disrupted but also the cyber-enabled perpetrator might gain publicity from his or her act—a common goal of such attacks. Distributed denial of service (DDoS) is a modified DoS where multiple attacks are launched simultaneously from various innocent client computers to a single target, flooding the computer server system and locking it up. DoS/DDoS attacks have less of an impact on financial institutions and are less devastating to the overall entity than the other forms of attack.

**16.2.7 Debit/Credit Card Cloning:** Debit/credit card cloning, or "skimming" as it is sometimes called, is a new technique whereby someone obtains your card details, copies them onto a bogus card and begins using the card. While card theft itself is not new, the manner in which the information is stolen is worth a look. Generally for debit card, the fraudster tells that the machine is not working and that they need to swipe the card on their machine. After you hand them your card they will swipe their debit machine and when you're busy putting in your PIN code they swipe it again on a card recorder. Security cameras or an accomplice looking over your shoulder collects the PIN code as you type it in the machine.

Fraudsters use a pocket sized device with a scanning slot. This device resembles a pager or even a legitimate credit card device, and the swiping can be done discreetly behind the counter or out of sight of the customer or other employees. Once all the information in the customer's card has been saved into the device with the intent to clone the information, it can be used to create a new card or to overwrite a stolen one.

The card recorder can be used to make a duplicate debit card that can be used at any automated bank machine. In this method it is virtually impossible to trace the offender. The criminal can also slowly take the money out of your account over time without you even knowing it. Most people don't find out they are being robbed until the end of the month when they receive their bank statement. By then the criminal would have made off with everything.

**16.2.8 Hacking:** "Hacking" is a crime, which entails cracking systems and gaining unauthorized access to the data stored in them. Hacking in simple terms means an illegal intrusion into a computer system and/or network. There is an equivalent term to hacking i.e. cracking, but from Indian laws perspective there is no difference between the term hacking and cracking. Every act committed towards breaking into a computer and/or network is hacking. Hackers write or use ready-made computer programs to attack the target computer. They possess the desire to destruct and they get the kick out of such destruction. Some hackers hack for personal monetary gains, such as stealing the credit card information, transferring money from various bank accounts to their own account followed by withdrawal of money. They extort money from some corporate giant threatening them to publish the stolen information which is critical in nature.

**16.2.9 E-mail Bombing:** It refers to sending a large number of emails to the victim resulting in the victim's email account or mail servers crashing.

**16.2.10 Data Diddling:** This attack involves altering raw data just before it is processed by a computer and then changing it back after processing is completed. Electricity boards in India have been victims to such data diddling programmes when private parties were computerizing their records.

**16.2.11 Logic Bombs:** Logic bombs are event dependent programmes. These programmes are created to do something only when an event (known as trigger event) occurs. Even some viruses can be termed as logic bombs because they lie dormant throughout the year and become active only on a particular date.

**16.2.12 Web Jacking:** Web Jacking occurs when someone forcefully takes control of a website (by cracking the password and later changing it). The actual owner of the website does not have any more control over what appears on the website.

**16.2.13 Money Laundering:** During the last two decades, IT and internet technologies have reached every nook and corner of the world. Internet has transformed the planet into a market place that never sleeps. Computer networks and Internet facilitate transfer of funds electronically between trading partners, businesses and consumers. This can be done in many ways like use of credit cards, Internet banking, e-cash, e-wallet, smart cards. In some other forms of computer-based e-money, there is no upper limit. This problem is further compounded by the fact that, in several countries, non-financial institutions are also allowed to issue e-money. Earlier, cross-border transactions were controlled by the central banks of respective countries. With the beginning of Internet commerce, the jurisdictional technicalities come into play and it is another area that is being exploited by the money launderers. The competence to transfer limitless amounts of money without having to go through strict checks makes cyber money laundering an attractive proposition.

The main objective of cyber crime guidelines is to prevent banking transactions from being used by criminals intentionally or unintentionally as an element of money laundering. Banks and financial institutions are the core targets or focus in anti-money laundering practices and combating of financial terrorism laws due to their vulnerability and adherence of these laws is necessary to combat money laundering. Money laundering reduces the amount of banks' business and causes fluctuations in the exchange rate. Money laundering can undermine the credibility of the banking system. Facilitating the activities of launderers even inadvertently can land the banks into problems with law enforcement agencies and also government.

**16.3 Control and Prevention of Electronic Crime in Banks**

In a first of its kind initiative in India to tackle cyber crime, police have taken the initiative to keep an electronic eye on the users of the various cyber cafes spread over the city. The Central Bureau of Investigation (CBI) and the Mumbai Police have recommended issuance of licenses to cyber café owners. Many countries, including India, have established Computer Emergency Response Teams (CERTs) with an objective to coordinate and respond during major security incidents/events. These organisations identify and address existing and potential threats and vulnerabilities in the system and coordinate with stakeholders to address these threats. Policy initiatives on cyber crime are as yet lethargic because of a general sense that it is nothing more than juvenile hackers out to have fun or impress someone. Prateek Bhargava, cyber law expert says, "There is huge potential for damage to national security through cyber attacks".

The internet is a means for money laundering and funding terrorist attacks in an organized manner. In the words of Pavan Duggal, Supreme Court Lawyer, "cyber crime is omnipresent and although cyber crime cells have been set up in major cities, most cases remain unreported due to lack of awareness". Cyber space security management has already become an important component of national security management, military related scientific security management and intelligence management all over the world. Future intrusions threatening our national security may not necessarily come from across the land frontier, or in air space or across maritime waters, but happen in cyberspace. Intelligence operations and covert actions will increasingly become cyber-based. It is important that our intelligence agencies gear themselves up to this new threat. It is, therefore, necessary to put in place a

'National Cyber Space Security Management Policy' to define the tasks, specify responsibilities of individual agencies with an integrated architecture.

Banks can use some specific information technology (IT) or information systems (IS) countermeasures to mitigate the risk of cyber-crime. Banks decide themselves their controlling and preventive measures. Electronic crime is fast and increasing due to the fact that evolution of technology. While evolution of IT is fast, the evolution of law is slow. Protection measures such as hardware identification; access controls software and disconnecting critical bank applications are required. However, it should be noted that computers do not commit crimes, the perpetrators' best advantage is ignorance of others. Proper internal controls reduce the opportunity for fraud. While a variety of countries are passing legislation relating to computer crime, the awareness of the situation is still low in India. To effectively tackle the problem, organizations needs to make the public aware of their experiences about cyber crime.

The Indian banking sector has recorded an impressive improvement in productivity over the last 15 years and many of the productivity/efficiency indicators have moved closer to the global levels. There has been a particularly discernible improvement in banks' operating efficiency in recent years owing to technology up-gradation and staff restructuring. With more technology based growth, the aspect relating to IT risks is a very critical issue. With the increased use of IT, there are attendant risks posed to the banks as well as their customers in terms of monetary loss, data theft, breach of privacy and banks need to be extremely cognizant of such risks. Empowering customers with technology-driven benefits is a big challenge. The challenge is to leverage technology optimally to balance growth, efficiency and risk management objectives.

# 17

# The Way Forward

India is ready to experience an average real gross domestic product (GDP) growth of 5.8 percent between 2007-50 and it is likely to grow to almost 90 percent of the size of the US economy by 2050, while in the short-term, the GDP growth was 8.2 percent in FY 2010-11 and projected to be 6.5 percent in FY 2012-2013. Over the last five years, India has ranked amongst the top three FDI destinations, taking its place after China and the United States.

The rural population of India remains significantly under-penetrated, and it is essential to leverage technology to reach this un-banked population. In emerging markets, banking reaches about 37 percent of the population, compared to a 50 percent penetration rate for mobile phones. For every 10,000 people, these countries have one bank branch and one ATM—but 5,100 mobile phones. RBI has emphasized the need to focus on spreading the reach of banking services to the un-banked population of India. Statistics state that only 37 percent of bank branches of scheduled commercial banks are in rural areas with only around 40 percent of the population holding bank accounts.

The pace of development for the Indian banking industry has been tremendous over the past decade. As the world reels under the global financial meltdown, India's banking sector has been one of the very few to actually maintain resilience while continuing to provide growth opportunities, a feat unlikely to be matched by other developed markets around the world. Recent time has witnessed the world economy develop serious difficulties in terms of collapse of banking and financial institutions and plunging demand. Over the last three decades, there has been a remarkable increase in the size, spread and scope of activities of banks in India. The business profile of banks has transformed dramatically to include non-traditional activities like merchant banking, mutual funds, new financial services and human resource development.

Recently, prospects became very uncertain causing recession in major economies. However, amidst all this chaos India's banking sector has been amongst the few to maintain resilience. A progressively growing balance sheet, higher pace of credit expansion, expanding profitability and productivity akin to banks in developed markets, lower incidence of nonperforming assets and focus on financial inclusion have contributed to making Indian banking vibrant and strong. Indian banks have begun to revise their growth approach and re-evaluate the prospects on hand to keep the economy rolling. The way forward for the Indian banks is to innovate to take advantage of the new business opportunities and at the same time ensure continuous assessment of risks.

A rigorous evaluation of the health of commercial banks, recently undertaken by the Committee on Financial Sector Assessment (CFSA) also shows that the commercial banks are robust and versatile. The single-factor stress tests undertaken by the CFSA divulge that the banking system can endure considerable shocks arising from large possible changes in credit quality, interest rate and liquidity conditions. These stress tests for credit, market and liquidity risk show that Indian banks are by and large resilient.

Thus, it has become far more imperative to contemplate the role of the banking industry in fostering the long-term growth of the economy. With the purview of economic stability and growth, greater attention is required on both political and regulatory commitment to long-term development programme.

Change is the only constant feature in this dynamic world and banking is not an exception. The changes staring in the face of bankers relates to the fundamental way of banking—which is going through rapid transformation in the world of today. Adjust, adapt and change should be the key mantra. The global meltdown started as a banking crisis triggered by the credit quality. Indian banks seem to have paced up in terms of credit quality. As technology ingrains itself in all aspects of a bank's functioning, the challenge lies in exploiting the potential for profiting from investments made in technology. A lot needs to be done on the technological front to keep pace with global economies.

The idea of creating bigger banks to take on competition sounds attractive but one must realise even the biggest among Indian banks are small by global standards. The lack of global scale for Indian banks came into sharp focus during the recent financial crisis which saw several international banks reneging on their funding commitments to Indian companies, but local banks could not step into the breach because of balance sheet limitations. The future would require banks to have increased business agility and operational efficiency, which makes the implementation of core banking systems (CBS) by banks increasingly important. Effective control and monitoring byte top management, lower business operation costs and instant availability of accurate data are some of the valuable bye products of core banking solutions.

Banks are increasingly beginning to recognize human resources as a possible area of core competence, and seek to pursue and retain the best talent in the industry. There is a realization that skill development is extremely important for staff retention as well as the quality of manpower, and most banks have in place a system of continuous professional learning. Transition from class banking to mass banking and increased customer focus is drastically changing the landscape of Indian banking. Technology is a bank's best friend in pursuit of productivity. As Indian financial markets mature over time, there is also a need for innovative instruments to deepen the market further. New channels (like ATM and mobile phones) allow transactions at a fractional cost. Investment in technology in the Indian banking industry is about half of international average.

In India the industry has moved to technology-based processing, it is still far from technology-based decision-making. The huge opportunity shows up in customer adoption rates of new channels. Only about half of active customers in metros use ATM. Adoption rates of other new channels are much lower. India could be a world leader in mobile banking. Estimates show that, with the latest development in technology, 20-30 percent of banking transactions could be on mobile phones by 2020. This could lead to a 10-fold productivity rise in the not-too-far future. Banks need to invest in such technology and experiment with ways to induce considerable customer adoption.

Suggestions range from micro saving and micro insurance initiatives, cash deposit machines, warehouse receipts, to prepaid cash cards, derivatives, interest rate futures and credit default swaps as a means to further the financial inclusion and expansionary process. Capital adequacy is seen as important to the stability of the banking system. The minimum capital to risk-weighted asset ratio (CRAR) in India as required by RBI is placed at 9 percent, one percentage point above the Basel II requirement. Public sector banks are further required to maintain a CRAR of 12 percent by the Government of India. The CRAR of SCBs under Basel I was placed at 13 percent and under Basel II of 14.2 percent as of end of March 2011.

Non-Banking financial companies (NBFCs) are fast emerging as an important segment of Indian financial system. Gradually, they are being recognised as complementary to the banking sector due to their customer-oriented services; simplified procedures; attractive rates of return on deposits; flexibility and timeliness in meeting the credit needs of specified sectors; etc. Consolidation of operations continues to remain an important factor for banks as they seek to improve their levels of efficiency and correspondingly profitability.

The massive un-banked population of India is a constant reminder of a task unfinished. Developments in the micro finance sector highlight that the solutions for the un-banked have to come at reasonable interest margins. These conflicting demands of wider coverage but at low cost can come only with a substantial productivity increase in the Indian Banking sector. Consolidation in the banking industry has remained crucial to ensuring technological progress, excess retention capacity, emerging opportunities and deregulation of various functional and product restrictions. Consolidation is unavoidable if Indian banks are to become a force to reckon with in the near future.

One must keep in mind that the largest bank of China is five times the size of the five largest banks of India. Consolidation will only work if the synergistic values between the consolidating organizations are greater than the sum of parts. A merger of big bank with a small bank benefits the big bank in terms of wider market reach and lower spending on branch expansion, improved access to trained manpower and geographic diversification of risks. Service standards on response time have a long way to go.

Customers can get a mortgage loan sanctioned within hours in many developed markets. The best in India would be in days. The public sector has an unprecedented HR challenge. They have to deal with massive retirements and massive recruitments at the same time. Their talent shortage is preventing them from offering investment advisory to their clients. This will weaken their franchise. Administrative overheads of some banks are high at 15 percent of the staff costs as against global average of 10 percent.

The scene in the Indian banking industry is changing; the various global economies have started showing signs of revival leaving behind them the worst recessionary phase and moving towards growth. The Prime Minister of India, during the recent platinum jubilee celebrations of Reserve Bank of India, has encouraged banks to be more innovative.

Some factors which may probably be the key drivers for Innovation in banking, keeping in mind customer expectations and behaviour changes are:

1. Competition between banks is going to be more severe in the coming years and with more private players waiting to step in, adoption of new technology has assumed added importance, especially for public sector banks. The key to success is adopting state-of-the-art technology and continuously accelerating business processes.
2. Investment and innovation in technology will result in further advancement in credit analytics systems that will help them assess customer behaviour and enhance portfolio profitability. Experience in matured markets has proven the value of credit bureaus in the development of consumer credit. With the possibility of more credit bureau's competing with CIBIL looming large, further advancement and innovation to quickly assess customer credit history will be a critical factor to provide convenience banking to customers. The day is not far away where you call up your bank for a loan, provide your UID/PAN number, your credit score verified, eligibility calculated and the processing is completed almost instantaneously and the loan amount gets credited to your account within 24 hours.

The 2011 Census is going to throw up interesting focus areas for banks. The demographics of our country, with 54 percent of the Indian population being under 25 years of age and 60 percent within 40 years of age, will be a key driver to create a large retail customer base. With increasing income levels and an annual GDP growth of 8.5-9 percent predicted for the next 2-3 years, this segment is a good target market to sell insurance, mutual funds, credit cards, etc.

With so much of talk about inclusive growth and focus on rural development, there is a considerable gap between demand and supply for all financial services, especially in rural segments. Almost 70 percent of the rural population does not have a bank account, 85 percent do not have access to credit and less than 10 percent have any kind of insurance (life, health, crop insurance etc.). More importantly, 60 percent of the rural poor still borrow from moneylenders, friends and other sources.

There is no dearth of areas where improvement in productivity is possible in Indian banks. As the Indian economy grows rapidly in size and influence over the next few decades, it is imperative to have a strong and dynamic banking sector supporting it. Many analysts claim that among the competing emerging economies, India's strength in banking will give it an edge. Indian banks are not yet ready to claim this recognition. But they certainly can.

# Bibliography

# Bibliography

Ahluwalia, M.S., *Second Generation Reforms in the Banks: Major Issues*, paper presented at the Bank Economists' Conference (January 2001), New Delhi.

Bhatt, Nitin, Thorat, Y.S.P (2001), "India' Regional Rural Banks: The Institutional Dimension of Reforms", *Journal of Microfinance*, Vol. 3, No.1.

Gopinath, S., Recent Development in Forex, Money and Government Securities Markets: Account and Outlook, *RBI Bulletin*, August 2005.

Government of India, *Banking Committee Report*, 1972.

——*Economic Survey* (various issues).

——Ministry of Law, Justice, and Company Affairs, *Constitution of India.*

Hashemi, S.M. (2000), 'Micro Credit in Rural Development; Beyond Safety Netting to Poverty Alleviation', CIRDAP Report (July).

Jadhav, Narendra, Central Bank Strategies, Credibility and Independence: Global Evolution and the Indian Experience, *RBI Occasional Papers,* 2003.

Jadhav, Narendra, Partha Ray, D. Bose and Indranil Sen Gupta, The Reserve Bank of India's Balance Sheet: Analytics and Dynamics of Evolution, *RBI Occasional Papers,* 2003.

Kaveri, V. S., Loan Default and Profitability of Banks, *IBA Bulletin,* January 2001.

Kohli, S.S., Indian Banking Industry: Emerging Challenge, *IBA Bulletin*, March 2001.

Kulkarni, R. V., Changing Face of Banking from Brick and Mortar Banking to E-banking, *IBA Bulletin,* January 2000.

Mahajan, Vijay (2005), 'Micro Finance to Livelihood Finance', *Economic and Political Weekly*, Volume XL, No. 41.

Malhotra, R.N., *Evolution of Financial System,* Nineteenth

Frank Moraes Memorial Lecture, Chennai, September 1990.

Metzer, S.R., Strategic Planning for Future Bank Growth, *The Banker's Magazine,* July-August 2000.

Mohan, Rakesh, Transforming Indian Banking: In Search of a Better Tomorrow. *RBI Bulletin*, 2003.

Nair, Tara S. (2005), 'The Transforming World of Indian Micro Finance', *Economic and Political Weekly*, April 23.

Rangarajan, C., *Issues in Monetary Management*, Presidential Address at the Indian Economic Conference, Calcutta, December 1988.

Reddy, Y.V., Financial Sector Reforms and RBI's Balance Sheet Management, *RBI Bulletin*, December 1997.

Reserve Bank of India, *Functions and Working of RBI,* Fourth Edition (1983).

——*Reserve Bank of India: Fifty Years (1935-85)*, 1985

——*Report of the Committee on Financial System* (Chairman: M. Narasimham), 1991.

——*Report of the Committee on Banking Sector Reforms* (Chairman: M. Narasimham), 1998.

——*Core Principles of Effective Banking Supervision*, 1999.

——*Report of the Working Group on Internet Banking* (Chairman: S.R. Mittal), 2001.

——*Reserve Bank of India: Functions and Working,* Reserve Bank Staff College, Chennai, 2001.

——*Report of the Working Group on Electronic Money*, 2002.

——*History of the Reserve Bank of India* (Volume III), 2005.

——*Report on Trend and Progress of Banking in India (2010-11)*, 2011.

——*Report on Currency and Finance* (various years).

——*Bulletins.*

——*Occasional Papers.*

——*Annual Report* (Various Issues).

Shetty, S.L. (2003), *Credit Flows to Rural Poor*, mimeo, EPW Research Foundation, Mumbai.

Sinha, Saurabh (1998), 'Micro Credit: Impact, Training and

Sustainability', Institute of Development Studies (IDS), Volume 29, No. 4, October, University Sussex, U.K.

Tarapore, S.S., *Domestic Debt Management Policy and Monetary Control*, 18th SEANZA Central Banking Course Lectures, Reserve Bank of India, Mumbai, 1990.

Thingalaya, N.K. (2000), *The Other Side of Rural Banking*, BIRD Publication, Lucknow.

Thorat, U., Developing Bond Markets to Diversify Long-Term Development Finance: Country Study of India, *Asia-Pacific Development Journal*, June 2002.

**Web Sites**

www.bankingombudsman.rbi.org.in
www.bcsbi.org.in
www.sbicaps.com
www.sbimf.com
www.sbidfhi.com
www.sbifactors.com
www.sbicard.com
www.sbilife.co.in
www.sbigeneral.in
www.sbisgcsl.co.in
www.sbigeneral.in
www.csb.co.in
www.dhanbank.com
www.federal-bank.com
www.karnatakabank.com
www.kvb.co.in
www.southindianbank.com
www.cityunionbank.com
www.ingvysyabank.com
www.tmb.in
www.jkbank.net
www.lvbank.com
www.nainitalbank.co.in
www.theratnakarbank.com

www.axisbank.co.in
www.dcbbank.com
www.hdfcbank.com
www.icicibank.com
www.indusind.com
www.kotak.com
www.yesbank.in
www.abnamro.com
www.americanexpress.com
www.bnpparibas.co.in
www.online.citibank.co.in
www.db.com
www.hsbc.co.in
www.standardchartered.co.in

# Index

# Index